Henry W. Foote

Thy Kingdom Come

Ten sermons on the Lord's prayer

Henry W. Foote

Thy Kingdom Come

Ten sermons on the Lord's prayer

ISBN/EAN: 9783337184056

Printed in Europe, USA, Canada, Australia, Japan

Cover: Foto ©Lupo / pixelio.de

More available books at **www.hansebooks.com**

THY KINGDOM COME:

𝔗en 𝔖ermons

ON THE LORD'S PRAYER.

PREACHED IN KING'S CHAPEL, BOSTON,

BY

HENRY WILDER FOOTE.

BOSTON:
ROBERTS BROTHERS.
1891.

PREFACE.

THESE Sermons were prepared for the Sunday morning services at KING'S CHAPEL with no thought of publication, and lack the careful revision which Mr. Foote always deemed necessary before printing.

Preached after a time of deep experience in his own life, they spoke to those who heard them of the spiritual realities in which he himself had been living; and it is hoped that any who, in quietness, seek to enter into near companionship with this little book, will find in it a like help and blessing.

F. E. F.

BOSTON, October, 1891.

CONTENTS.

SERMON		PAGE
I.	Lord, Teach us to Pray	9
II.	Our Father Which Art in Heaven	35
III.	Hallowed be Thy Name	57
IV.	Thy Kingdom Come	79
V.	Thy Will be Done	101
VI.	Our Daily Bread	127
VII.	I. Forgiveness. — The Divine Side	139
VIII.	II. Forgiveness. — The Human Side	159
IX.	Lead Us not into Temptation	185
X.	But Deliver Us from Evil	209

LORD, TEACH US TO PRAY.

I.

"LORD, TEACH US TO PRAY."

And it came to pass, that, as he was praying in a certain place, when he ceased, one of his disciples said unto him, Lord, teach us to pray, as John also taught his disciples. — LUKE xi. 1.

THUS Saint Luke leads us into our Lord's Prayer. The Gospel according to Saint Matthew, you will remember, gives us the same great words of prayer as a part of the Sermon on the Mount. "But thou, when thou prayest, enter into thy closet, and when thou hast shut thy door, pray to thy Father which is in secret. ... When ye pray, use not vain repetitions, as the heathen do ... for your Father knoweth what things ye have need of, before ye ask him. After this manner therefore pray ye;" and then follows the prayer which, the more one studies its infinite depth of meaning, we see more and more to be at once the simplest and the most profound form of human words.

It is very natural that we should find this prayer of our Lord spoken by him not only in that Sermon on the Mount, which is, in a manner, the condensing of his gospel into one shining focus, but when his disciples want to be taught, as in our text. Doubtless before he led others into the paths of its supplications, which have since been trodden, like the aisles of ancient cathedrals, by uncounted prayerful feet, but which then were new and strange ways, unfrequented even by those who really sought to pray, — he first travelled them himself. They asked him to teach them as they saw the light in his face as he turned from his own prayers back to the common world in which they were; and they wanted to catch the glow of that divine fire, — to learn the secret of that communion. The strongest enforcement of his teaching about prayer is in the fact that he has himself tried it and *knows* whereof he speaks.

What else, indeed, is the life of Jesus Christ, if it be not, supremely, the visible expression of the duty which calls us to prayer, the renewal which is in prayer, the answer which is bestowed upon prayer? Whether it be in the consecration of the deep moments in his ministry when, at each point of crisis, he withdrew into the mountain alone and passed the night alone in prayer to his Father, or when he girded his spirit anew for great works of healing or mercy by lifting it from the heaven in which it always was to the heaven above it, or when he met the supreme hour in his life-work by bending in Gethsemane to take the cup whose bitter portion his Father gave him to drink of, — in all, his divinest moments manifest themselves to us through this act of prayer, as it were a window. The moments when he seems to come closest to us, yet seems most above us, are those when his soul blends in light and love with his Father's spirit, and we say, "Behold! he prayeth!"

So, then, that question asked by the disciples as by children coming to a wiser friend and helper, "Lord, teach us to pray," is brought home to us in the most affecting way by the persuasion of our Lord's example upon our loving obedience, and in the most convincing way by the clear shining in him of the truth of that spiritual law which lies at the heart of his religion, — that prayer is the living way open between our human spirits and the Divine Spirit.

I want to ask you to try with me, in some of our Sunday mornings together, to enter really into the heart of the meaning of this mighty prayer of our Christian faith as we only can do by pondering it deeply, sentence by sentence. I said it was at once the simplest and the most profound form of human words. Yet the fact that all of us have learned to say it, that the youngest child is not thought too young to be taught it, that every word in it is a simple word, may easily hide from us the infinite depth and height that is in it. Each sentence in it is transparently clear as the purest water — even the water of life; and as the clearness of a stream hides its depth, so I think we may easily fancy that we can sound this which is far beyond the reach of any merely earthly plummet. It would be possible for a person to imagine that he had got beyond the use of anything so familiar, so commonplace, as the Lord's Prayer, who never had *really* learned to say it at all. And the Lord's Prayer is not only infinitely deeper than the shallowness of any merely superficial thoughts about it, it is also far larger than to be only the expression of the gentle, pleading side of the character of Christ, — the breathing of the religious *sentiment* of Christianity. As a drop of water contains forces which, set loose, are akin to the thunderbolt and the earthquake, so the secrets of uttermost human need, of intensest human passion, and of the powers of Divine omnipotence, are all locked up in this mighty prayer which we have from our Master, Christ, — which we have from him because it was first in his own heart, with all its depths and heights and powers. If only we can be empowered to unlock these divine forces of strength and peace so as to bring them to bear prevailingly on our own spirits, filling them with the spirit of Jesus Christ!

"As he was praying in a certain place, when he ceased, one of his disciples said unto him, Lord, teach us to pray, as John also taught his disciples."

Yet at the very beginning the disciple is met by questions which strike at the root of the very idea of prayer itself. To pray is so natural an expression of human need and human aspiration that there is no record of any people among whom there has not been some method of addressing the unseen powers which they have worshipped, with appeals for succor or thanks for safety. Or if any contrary record has been found, the exception is only sufficient to prove the rule. To believe in the effect of such supplication belongs to the simple conditions of society which are its truest conditions; and only the artificial conditions which result from a highly complex social order give birth to doubt and disbelief of the reality of this vital relation between the spirit of man and the Divine Spirit. But these artificial conditions are exactly those of the world in which we are to-day; and since the questions which touch this vital matter live and breathe in the atmosphere which is our breath of life, we cannot help meeting them. They lie across the very threshold of our thoughts of prayer. At the threshold, then, we must pause to confront them for a moment, before we enter the Holy Place where there surely await us strength and peace.

The first "lion in the way" that meets us is the modern conception of law, eternal, universal, as leaving no place in the universe for prayer in the proper sense of the word. Not that the hard and inflexible sides of life are more grim and fatalistic in their bearing now than they were in the day when Jesus opened a living fountain of prayer for men. The cold of winter was as terrible on the snowy heights of Lebanon as to-day in the Arctic wave which engulfs a shuddering continent. The scorching heat of the Jordan Valley smote the disciples of John with pitiless fervor, even while he taught them. The same stars looked down with steely gleam from their fathomless spaces. The cruelties and hardnesses of human life were less softened by pity, — seemed more ruled by an iron fate than now. "John taught his disciples" to pray, and they prayed even in a world where the savage daughter of Herodias was suffered to dance his head off from his body; and the disciples of Jesus prayed in a world which was suffered to nail the holy one upon the cross, and by their prayer changed the face of that cruel, godless world. Yet I would not make light of the fact that the modern conceptions of the vast universal order do re-enforce the difficulties with which (God knoweth) *life as it is*, in its hardnesses and its pains, bears heavily upon our spirits.

The researches of physical science bring out in grander and grander outline, whichever way we look, the sublime idea of an Order immense beyond our power to measure, fixed beyond our power to change. Shining among the farthest specks of light, which are really worlds, keeping their appointed watch in their eternal orbits; written on every atom as it conforms to immutable laws of combination and proportion; beneath all the grand phenomena of the natural world, are deciphered indications of the Divine method of governing the universe. They give us a far juster and higher conception of it, a far clearer intellectual picture than former generations had. They seem to lift us above the thin film of atmosphere which wraps about our tiny earth-ball with a warm, hazy mantle, into the higher ether. But how cold and thin an air is that for faith to breathe!

But is it legitimate to infer from all this that God has so placed this huge framework of material laws *between* himself and his children, as a great gulf across which no human voice can cry so loud as to obtain an answer? Is the universe so subject to material laws that prayer can never avail within this vast environment? And shall we go the one step beyond this, and hold that spiritual things also follow an unvarying and an invariable order?

Doubtless, yes, so far as *this*,— that nothing can happen contrary to the eternal purposes of God, which purposes reveal themselves to us in law. But the mistake, it seems to me, of those who lay such emphasis — often with a truly religious spirit — upon the omnipotence of law, lies in divorcing it from the thought of the living God. We do not spell the word rightly in our minds if we let ourselves forget that law, mighty though it be, is only the constant expression of the will of One, a veritable Person, who is mightier. The hope of philosophers is that beneath all the laws of the physical universe they shall one day discover a higher law uniting them all. Is it not contrary to right reason to believe that such a higher law, while comprehending in its grasp all the other facts of the universe, would exclude the great fact of *prayer?* You believe that God is a Being, personal in the most vital sense of the word, who has ordered all the laws of the universe in the highest wisdom; how can you help believing that the instinct and impulse which moves the heart in the most intense moments of our life to flutter up toward Him in petition, — nay, rather, to rise by a natural gravitation to Him as its source, as "fire ascending seeks the sun," — how, I say, can you help believing that this divine instinct has a place in the great system of his providential order? He has so ordered his world, you say, that certain events shall follow in regular sequence. But what prevents you from believing that prayer shall be one event in that sequence; and, if so, that the final issue shall be shaped in part by that prayer? I believe that the true science will more and more come to accept this large view, and so will more and more come into accord with the simple heart of faith. For faith is surely right in feeling that if the voice of prayer were hopelessly silenced, the Father, loving and pitiful, revealed to us in the Gospel of Christ, would be gone from us; and not only so, but every personal attribute which we ascribe to Him would be dissolved away from the inscrutable mystery in which the thought of God would elude our most anxious quest.

Do I, then, mean to say that our prayers *must* be answered according to their request? By no means necessarily so. It may comport better with the will of God that they should be answered quite otherwise. I see not, indeed, how those who know the history of such human lives as have been lived in this world a thousand and a thousand times, can doubt that men *have* received such answers as could not be explained except by the presence of the intervening God. I think there must be many of us here to-day who are not ignorant what it is, at times of deep religious experience, to feel thrilled and awed by a sense that when the soul opened itself willingly to the Divine influence a guidance was felt, a grace was given, which we could only understand when we saw that the human spirit ascending was met by the Divine Spirit descending in answer.

But "the first condition of prayer is, that it shall be really offered to *God*, — that is, to the highest and purest will of which he who prays has any conception. It must mean desire not to overrule, but to be overruled by Him." A selfish wish, even if thrown out in that form, is still selfishness praying to itself. He who gave us the Lord's Prayer, with its trustful voicing of our great human needs, has shown us the spirit which should underlie all our prayer, when in his own hour of trial he cried, "Nevertheless, Father, not as I will, but as thou wilt!"

"In Christ's sense, Christian prayer addresses primarily not God's omnipotence at all, but his spiritual nature. . . . Prayer is . . . the chief method by which the eager and short-sighted and imperfect mind gradually learns to purify itself in the flame of Divine love. People talk and think as if prayer only meant bringing *pressure to bear for private purposes* on the Power which touches the secret springs of life. But in Christ's teaching it means bringing Divine influences to bear on these private purposes, so as to extinguish or transform them."

Do I, then, mean to say that it is only fitting for us to ask for *spiritual* gifts or blessings? This thought is, it seems to me, another "lion in the way," which prevents many a soul from finding in prayer the comfort and help they might naturally hope for. That which seems, at first sight, a peculiarly spiritual view of the whole subject, hinders instead of helping the spiritual benefit.

It mingles (do you say?) an element of selfishness in that communion with the Unseen which should be absolutely pure and unselfish, if we mix with it the thought of any temporal advantage we may be desiring. This has a specious sound, but is it so in fact? Again we turn to the great prayer of our Lord for light; and we certainly find that it touches the great needs of the life where we are. It speaks as the voice of human need uttering itself to Him who is able to answer our need. Now, manifestly, we do not need *only* spiritual benefits. No day can pass without your feeling aware that you want some earthly blessing, all the way from the gain of some prosperity which would give new ease to mind and heart, to the enriching in love or friendship which is so fine a treasure added to your nature that you can hardly separate it in your thought from purely spiritual gifts. If you ought not to pray for these things you must leave all such thoughts pertaining to our common life outside the door of the closet where we pray. But what an inference is this! It is simply saying that the larger part of our life is outside the sphere which we expect God to touch. How can it otherwise than follow that we shall come to regard the interests and occupations which fill so much of our waking thoughts as beyond the region of his care, — lying entirely in the earth's shadow? In other words, we shall remove the chief obstacle which prevents our selfishness from becoming entirely selfish, — the most spiritual element which we can mingle with our desires to purge away their earthiness and their worldliness. Do you find, as a fact, that you are more spiritual-minded when you practise on this theory than when you bring prayer into the circle of your daily life? Are not your requests for spiritual blessings apt to become faint and far between if you painfully winnow out from them every hint of the most real wants which confront you every hour and engross time and mind and heart?

In this age of the world, when the chimneys of your factories blur the sky with their smoke, when the noise of your business drowns the silence till you cannot hear yourself think, there must be slight danger of bringing the thought of God too close to the sphere of practical life.

And the Christian conception of God — which

is the only conception in which our intellect and our heart can find reconciliation — will not let us hold any other idea but this.

"Though the highest prayers are prayers for the fulfilment of God's will, whatever it be, . . . there is so much spiritual education in the habit of intimate communion with God, — that is, of constantly bringing our human desires into a presence in which nothing merely selfish can long remain, — that we are induced to pour out our hearts even to their most childish wishes before Him, by the assurance that it is often His will to give what we ask *because* we ask it, even where it would not have been God's purpose to give it if we had not asked it. Is there any inconsistency between the belief that there are some human prayers which God grants in order to draw closer the tie between Him and man, and the belief that the true object of prayer is to lift man up to God, to subdue the human will to the Divine? . . . No! because the Christian teaching impresses on us, not that man is to be extinguished in God, but that he must be utterly willing and desirous to surrender himself to God.

Hence he is to have a self to surrender,—a permanent self to mould into the Divine image, but never to lose."

The highest view of life is the truest. Only when we regard it as God's gift to us, and its privileges as ways of serving Him, do we know how to use them aright. Whatever life gives us, then, of good, comes from God. Whatever good we desire will be given us by Him, if indeed we obtain it. This being so, how can we but ask Him for what we want? The house whose walls you are rearing, the business enterprise which fills your thoughts, the welfare of the friend, the child, who is dearer than life to you,—shall we not tell Him that we depend upon His favor for these? But, you say, it is not seemly to ask for what He already knows our wish for; He will give it, if it is best for us, without our asking. Why, the point is, that you are asking it already by trying to get it,—knocking persistently at a door of gain, which you are trying with all your human might to open. Will you not ask in a higher way, by lifting up the object of your desire into the purer atmosphere of spiritual communion, — baptizing your *wish* into conscious *prayer?*

Nor have we a right, either, to think that our request has no effect upon the mind of God.

There is nothing contrary to a true philosophy, as I have said, in holding that prayer is a part of His law, fully understood. That He is a Person implies that He will hear his child. It may be that He will answer according to the letter of the prayer; it may be that He will not so answer. But if you have prayed in the right spirit of submission and love and trust, or even with a great yearning of your struggling heart to win such a spirit, it is certain — it must be a law of the Divine nature itself — that He will answer in ways according to your true necessity, and that He will answer *because you pray.* "*Ask,*" said Christ, "and ye shall receive; *seek*, and ye shall find; *knock*, and it shall be opened." And only so.

But manifestly, in saying this we imply that no temporal benefit, however high or true, exhausts our thought of what we need from God.

Our deepest wants are those which touch no other human spirit, — which no outward possession can satisfy. The soul meets problems of duty, and our unaided wisdom is not able to solve them. We need an absolute standard of right to regulate our conduct. How shall we obtain it, unless by turning our thoughts to the Highest? We rise from the self-flattery which misleads and from the flattery of others which blinds us, to Him who "trieth the heart," and we are at once in a different position. The very fact that we have assumed such an attitude of spirit must avail much. In prayer, ordinary things fall away from the soul and leave us face to face with the things of the spirit. In prayer comes that holy calmness of soul in which its still depths reflect truly our responsibleness and our actual life, with their grave, clear outlines undistorted. In prayer, and in prayer alone, the spirit touches its highest reach of spiritual life, and is attuned to receive the light and strength without which the human spirit in its uttermost times of need must droop and fail.

> "Be not afraid to pray; to pray is right.
> Pray, if thou canst, with hope; but ever pray,
> Though hope be weak, or sick with long delay;
> Pray in the darkness, if there be no light.
> Far is the time, remote from human sight,
> When war and discord on the earth shall cease;
> Yet every prayer for universal peace
> Avails the blessed time to expedite.
> Whate'er is good to wish, ask that of Heaven,
> Though it be what thou canst not hope to see;
> Pray to be perfect, though material leaven
> Forbid the spirit so on earth to be;
> But if for any wish thou dar'st not pray,
> Then pray to God to cast that wish away." [1]

We need, too, to pray in order to deepen our thankfulness to God. We go on from day to day, often almost without thought of Him to whom we owe the gift of our happiness and the blessing which He has hidden even in our pain. Prayer gives us time to think, and brings a light above the earth into our thought. We pause on that mount of vision, and as the soul draws closer to God His presence fills all things with good. The beauty of the world of nature in its spotless robe of winter white, is as His new creation. The deep happiness which lies

[1] Hartley Coleridge.

at the heart of so many hours of every human life has a deeper undertone of blessedness. And even grief and suffering, in the light of prayer, turn to our eyes the "silver lining" of their cloud. The soul may resort to prayer from the sense of its weakness, its bitter need; but when the spirit of prayer is with it, it will pass from seeking into gratitude, and will give thanks, though it be with Christ, over "the cup which is not wine, but sorrow, fear, and blood."

Through gratitude to communion! The highest end of prayer is to bring us to that living intercourse with the Living Father of our spirits which is intended to be the greatest joy of the soul. The prayer that seeks for some earthly blessing or some spiritual gift from God, in a right spirit, is undoubtedly a true prayer. If we do not begin by such seeking, it may be that we shall never truly pray at all. But the prayerful spirit learns to rise high above such conditions of intercourse with God, into pure communion with Him as the Fountain of its spiritual life. Petition becomes a devout desire to rest in Him, to trust Him utterly. We come to ask less and less of Him for ourselves and for those dearest to us, — except that he will give us of *Himself*.

The prayer which Christ has given us as the measure and rule of our worship and our faith, begins and ends with God, — " Our Father . . . whose is the kingdom, power, and glory." Surely, friends, we ought to ask that this may be supremely the *habit* of our soul. To be real and yet at the same time to be submissive, — wrestling with the Lord yet waiting upon the Lord, — our prayer must breathe forth from calm, deep places, where the spirit of prayer has brooded long, like the dove upon the waters. It need not always be in spoken words; hardly need it always even be syllabled in the thought. Yet thought and words will be the garment in which the deep spiritual consciousness which is the inner essence of prayer will naturally clothe itself.

Without a spirit of trusting confidence, what can lend wings or life to the prayer which strives to rise heavenward? Its home is on the earth, among cold dispositions and unspiritual thoughts. But prayer *with* faith is the laying hold by the spirit on things beyond the senses' grasp. It is drawing near to God as our Heavenly Friend, our Father. "Prayer," said Coleridge, "is faith passing into act."

Who would not desire to bring the Divine Life, the Divine Presence, into our daily consciousness, to transfigure the common things about us by that light?

OUR FATHER WHICH ART IN HEAVEN.

II.

OUR FATHER WHICH ART IN HEAVEN.

After this manner, therefore, pray ye : Our Father which art in heaven. — MATT. vi. 9.

"AFTER this manner!" When Christ bids his followers pray thus, he tells us in substance that the few sentences of the Lord's Prayer are the *essence* of *all* prayer. Since prayer addresses *God*, he teaches us first of all how to think of Him; since prayer speaks to Him of our wants, he teaches us how we are to think of ourselves; and since these things are the very things which most concern us to know, he is really teaching us in this prayer the sum of all theology, as well as how to pray.

The first words of this mighty prayer lift us at once to the highest level.

Christianity has well been called "a dispensation of encouragement." The principles of the gospel and the mighty life of Christ answer through and through to our need to be braced and heartened in the religious life. And what is the breath of life of this Christian Gospel, so alive with hope? Is it not this, that it is possible for men to know and to love God, as children know their father? From the Sermon on the Mount to the deep words spoken at the Last Supper, from the whole spirit of his Gospel, and from that one solitary Life which includes all this while it is itself more than all, arises the same voice as the key-note: God, our Father.

It was not always so. When Jesus taught his disciples to call God by that name, he gave them not only the greatest thought, but what was a new thought. Their religion, the religion of the Jews, knew Him by noble names, presented Him in sublime and living conceptions. But in all the references to the Supreme One in the Old Testament, " He is mentioned just seven times as a Father, — five times as the Father of the Hebrew people, twice as sustaining that relation to individuals. Of these two intimations that God is the Father of individual men, one is a promise to David that God will be a Father to his son Solomon; the other is a prediction that by and by men will pray to God, calling him Father,—a prediction fulfilled in this prayer. For there is no record of any prayer in the Old Testament in which God is addressed as Father."[1] So, then, when Christ taught them to know the Mighty, the Eternal One by that name, he opened to them a new world of tender pieties and warm and living faith.

Yet I suppose that there are many persons who, in the theory of what virtuous living is, reduce religion solely to the practice of good morals, from the fear of mixing with it something ecstatic or extravagant or absurd. Just as our American atmosphere has little of soft haze and transfiguring shadows in it, but is hard and clear in outline, a dazzling overflow of pure, dry light, so our religious climate is unfavorable to anything mysterious, or which transcends the senses; and there is many a man who has a clear insight into the duties which concern living well on this earth, whose horizon has a per-

[1] Washington Gladden.

fectly defined, hard outline, beyond which he does not know or care to go, and which shuts down on this side of the whole range of spiritual duties and affections.

And yet, that we *need* something more, I suppose that the coolest brain and the most clear-sighted mind among us all would be the quickest to admit. For they ought to know most powerfully how many hindrances stand in the way of our acting as if we were moral machines, which needed only to be wound up for every cog and wheel to run in order. Is it so easy, then, for you to keep the little, petty things of life from marring your peace? Is it so easy to prevent the unworthiness of those whom you trusted, the selfishness of those whom perhaps you have labored for and sacrificed yourself for, from clouding your faith in human goodness? Is it so easy to keep your own faith in the law of goodness, when you are tempted to be unjust, unkind, impure? There is no one who has really lived at all who does not know that we need the most transforming and empowering motives that can be brought into our souls, just to help us do the least, common thing that we have to do every day, rightly and well. The way of the world has too often been the contrary, — narrow the minds that have to do with narrow things; keep the poor ignorant; exclude the light from the ground-story of our civilization; let those who have to do drudgeries do them in a menial spirit. But not so Jesus Christ. He recognizes that the mind will only fulfil the lowest possible task when it has been filled full with the greatest possible thought. And so he calls men, all men, to open their whole being to the transforming possession of the thought of God and what follows therefrom, — love to Him and to His children. That is a mighty phrase of Dr. Chalmers, in which he speaks of "the expulsive power of a great affection." Who is he so poor as not to know something of what that means, — how the love of one human soul for another will drive out the baser passions that lurk like creeping things in the dark recesses of the human spirit? In the presence of that radiant angel shining with the light of God's countenance, in the love of parent and child, of husband and wife, how do selfishness, hardness, uncleanness, shrink away! Now, religion would not be religion if it did not give us the greatest affection of all, a supreme spirit, of which these finest and purest earthly relations are signs and illustrations, — something which would bring the most spiritual motive to bear on us in the same way as these highest and best motives in our common life are brought to bear on that to ennoble it. There must be, then, even if you do not understand it, — even if this side of religion seems to you mystical and incomprehensible, — still there must be some real and vital sense in which we can speak of God as our Father. If there are common misconceptions of the nature of the love of God, it behooves us the more to ask what is its real character. If there are practical difficulties in the way of our loving Him, we should seek the more to remove them.

This great spiritual affection which Christ names love to God, so far from being ecstatic or extravagant, is the chief safeguard in religion against excess. It is the very foundation on which all true and rational religion must be built. But it must be admitted that the simple and natural understanding of the great commandment has been rendered far more difficult by the erroneous methods of interpreting it pursued by great schools of Christian theology. And one or another of these partial definitions of what the love of God means do to this hour, I believe, profoundly color the ideas on this subject of many persons who belong to the most modern, most rational schools of thought. We are heirs of the past to a greater degree than we are aware. From the Middle Ages we inherit the unconscious tendency to measure spiritual feeling by extravagance of expression; from two centuries of New England parentage, an inborn zest for theological subtleties; and either way, we hold too narrow an idea of what this spiritual affection is. We need to go back to Jesus Christ, and look at it in his light. And when we thus bring the New Testament spirit to bear upon the interpretation of the great commandment, we at once find that in its genuine and true and Scriptural sense, love to God is not a mere *sentiment* dependent upon the happy possession of a glowing temperament, nor only a fervid expression of devout feeling called into being, quickened by supernatural grace; these are only special manifestations of it in partial forms. But underlying them and manifesting itself in many other ways also quite as true and as worthy, it exists as a great persuasive principle of life, vitalizing the whole being in the soul which religion has entered as a power. Jesus Christ does not say, " Thou shalt love Him with all thy heart," and stop there, but " with all thy heart and with all thy soul and with all thy mind and with all thy strength," — that is, with all that is in you of affection, of spiritual aspiration, of understanding, of active service. Why should we suppose for a moment that love to God is any less wide or less real an affection than love in any of our earthly relations? Interpret its breadth by these fair and dear ties which you know so well. You do not love your parent or your child with a mere sentiment, pleased with pleasant thoughts about them; you love them with your *life*, — the whole of what you are at your best. Perhaps you hardly ever put before yourself in set thoughts whether you love them or not. The affection is too deep and thorough to be thought about or talked about; it simply *is*. With your heart, yes; but with your soul too, for it is the immortal part in them which is closest to you; with the mind, ever busy with thoughtfulness for them; with the strength, that where you really love is eager to spend itself in doing something for them. Reason from this to the quality of love for our Father in heaven. Whether its prevailing character will be emotional or moral, intellectual or practical, will depend on the general bent of the individual, — what we call the personal temperament; but to all alike it belongs to love Him with what they *are*.

It is true, indeed, that here we reason only from analogy, and dimly. We cannot reduce to nothing the mystery which separates the human from the Divine. He retires before our thought into the awful depths of His infinite nature. How shall man dare to commune with Him who hideth Himself behind the brightness of the firmament, and whom the heaven of heavens cannot contain? But we carry this fitting sense of awe too far if we account it impossible in any way to hold communion with Him. For there are yearnings within the soul which were created that they might be satisfied; and unless the signs of His lovingkindness which fill the world of every one of us called forth an answering feeling, we should be dull of heart indeed. In whatever other ways the intercourse of the human spirit with the Infinite Spirit differs from that of man with man, it does so not least in this, — that the eye, the voice, the hand, which are so large a part of your friend, are absent when you hold converse with the Father of spirits "in spirit and in truth." But it may be a far closer, more real relation than that which you hold to your friend when absent. Though the farthest seas roll between, and for years you have been parted, you love him, you shape your life with reference to him.

It would be strange if it were impossible to do as much when it is with Him who filleth all things, and reads and knows your most hidden thought, that you have to do.

In one regard, indeed, this spiritual attitude toward the Supreme Ruler of our life and Father of our spirits has a manifest advantage over your love for your friend. There is something in the personal visible presence of one you care for, which forbids any analysis of character. You do not half know the person whom you love. Seldom do you appreciate the qualities wrapped up in a beloved person until the stern messenger comes who takes away your companion, though it be with strong crying and tears, and leaves you with what was really your friend, — the character for the first time truly known.

But this personal attitude of love and trust toward God as our Father in heaven must always be largely and may be almost wholly manifested toward the *qualities* of the Divine nature. It has to do with the affections and principles of our nature in their highest sense.

It is an attitude of the whole being, "heart and soul and mind and strength," toward the qualities which are attributes of God. And so we have a right to say that many a soul, by recognizing and obeying as Divine impulses those noble instincts which God has implanted in every human heart, has been loving Him even though it knew it not. When, for example, men have been loyal to the natural sense of justice which bade them deal honorably with their neighbor, it shows that they love a quality which eternally belongs to the Holy and Just One. Or when they are obedient to that higher hospitality which ministers to the needy, the oppressed, the forsaken, they show their love for that principle of love which *is* the very heart of God's own nature. You are faithful, perhaps, in the plain tasks of your common domestic cares, bringing with them the spirit of self-surrender, and receiving them as opportunities sent you by your Heavenly Father; you have learned something of the secret which so transfigures trial and privation as to make them even set off by their dull foil the beauty of faithful character. Is not this some sign of childlike love for His character and of trust in the fatherly dealings of Him who "maketh everything beautiful in His time"?

Yes! it is a divine, a blessed decree, that in obeying the best impulse of the heart towards what is holy and good and true, we are led into sympathy with Him in whom all perfections are in their fulness.

The relation of the child with the Father is something more, when it is perfected, when it comes to the knowledge of itself, than loyal affection for the abstract qualities which are in the Divine Being. In order that the religion of our lives may be kindled into a living flame, we need to feel that these qualities exist in a Person whom we can call by the fatherly name, of whom we may dare to think with the filial thought. The affection which we feel for Justice or Truth or Love, as abstract principles, is but cold in comparison with that for One who is just and true and loving.

So we come to see the force of those words of our prayer, "which art." The need of our lives and of our souls is to feel a living conviction of the real and living Being of God, as the One in whom existence is in all its fulness, — not One simply for us to read of or to hear of, but to know as the Person without whom the universe would be empty for us, without whom we could not live, in whom we shall find all beside that we love and long for, — Our Father, the Living God.

If we can but know Him as that, if we can but love Him as that, what a meaning will it not put upon the face of all things!

The cry of the soul is always for the Living God. And what is every breathing forth of our desire for succors from the unseen source of strength, but a witness that He is one who will answer? Is there nothing which speaks with proof of the attributes and the character of the Father of pity and God of all comfort in these voices of the soul? The earnest longing of the spirit newly roused to the sense that it is His child, the plaintive supplication of the wounded heart in the freshness of a great sorrow, the upliftings which sometimes visit the soul like a tidal wave and sweep it on their surging crest to spiritual thoughts far beyond its reach at common times, — to deny that these things witness to God is to strike a blow at the truth of human consciousness. Only they who have never felt these experiences can doubt their power of revelation.

The heart that glows with the new love of a regenerated child of God knows Him; the eyes that look upward through tears, see beyond the veil that hides Him from us; the soul that reaches out after heaven lays hold on that which it seeks. There are moments in such spiritual life when the soul seems to pass beyond the boundaries of space and time, and feels that it touches the Infinite Presence, and can even understand some hint of the meaning of our Saviour when he said, "I and my Father are one."

If you have gone thus far with me, you will feel that each word in this great sentence of our prayer is full of light, which to fully focus for us would ask more time for each word than we have here together. Let us look at them only briefly, then, before I close.

Mr. Maurice has well said that "much of the practical difficulty of the prayer lies in the first word of it. How can we look round on the people whom we habitually feel to be separated from us by almost impassable barriers, . . . and then teach ourselves to think that in the very highest exercise of our lives they are associated with us; that when we pray we are praying for them and with them; that we cannot speak for ourselves without speaking for them; that if we do not carry their sins to the throne of God's grace, we do not carry our own; that all the good we hope to obtain there belongs to them just as much as to us. . . . Yet all this is included in the word 'our;' till we have learned so much we are but spelling at it, we have not learned to pronounce it."

Have we so learned, any one of us, dear friends? For if we have hard thoughts about any in our hearts; if we find it difficult to hold them graciously and tenderly in our remembrance as we rise to the great thought of God; if we fail to grasp the sublime conception of "the whole family in heaven and earth" which is named of Him, we can hardly pass this portal of our Lord's Prayer into the deeper meaning of the sanctuary within. We do not really pray to Him unless we are willing to kneel, as it were, on the outer step of His temple, beside the publican and the sinner. We can hardly dare to call him Father, unless we will also call them our brethren.

But there is not only a lesson of humility and of charity for us when we begin to say "*Our* Father," — there is infinite hope and cheer. For if we all come *together* before him, we may well feel upborne by the praying might of all who are higher than we on the shining ladder that leads to the foot of His throne, — His saints and faithful children, all that great company who are joined in the praises of the Te Deum.

If our prayers for *ourselves* form a part of the Divine government of the individual, our prayers for one another surely must form a part of the Divine government of society.

Be not afraid to lift your thought of those you love, your care for them, into the light of God's presence. To pray for them is often the only thing you can do for them. And surely the scope of these opening words of this great prayer does not stop at the horizon-line between earth and heaven. If there be any petition in it which God's angels do not need to utter, it is not these words, "Our Father." Dante represents the great company of the redeemed whom he saw in his vision of Paradise bursting forth in this prayer together. They are the only human words great enough and high enough for us to imagine on those purified lips. But we can think — and we have a right to think — that through that prayer, blending *us* even with their thought of God, they reach out to us to lift our need into His light. Shall we not also feel that we can blend them too with our deepest prayer, — that our love and our sorrow can reach up after them and find them in His presence, and can ask for them and win for them more of His light, more of His peace?

"Our Father which art in heaven." The closing words of this name by which we know Him are surely not the least part of our knowledge. "In heaven," — how the clear shining of that thought dissipates like a beam of morning light all the mists of darkness which have gathered about low and unworthy conceptions of what God is! All the old idols fell from their altars at this word which reveals the Living God dwelling in light, inaccessible and full of glory. Is the peril wholly past with any of us? Do you never set up an image in your own heart, of wealth or power or success or pleasure, and worship it? For if you do, let your prayer to your Father in heaven tone your soul to a worthier worship. If the real prayer of your soul, if that to which you really bend your life, is less than the loftiest and purest and holiest vision to which you can lift your thought, it is not the Being, awful in height and purity, whom Christ teaches us to name Our Father. "Who art in heaven." We may not know *where* heaven is; to figure forth its glories in our poor human speech, or even to shadow them forth in our dim thought, we may not dare. But we know that where God is, heaven is. There is something of it in every pure soul, in every faithful life. The holy ones who have passed from such a life here have "breathed free the blessed air of heaven, and knew their native air." And we are called to rise to this level of desire and hope. "Beloved," says the Apostle, "now are we the sons of God, and it doth not yet appear what we shall be; but we know that when He shall appear we shall be like Him; for we shall see Him as he is. And every man that hath this hope in him purifieth himself, even as He is pure."

HALLOWED BE THY NAME.

III.

HALLOWED BE THY NAME.

Hallowed be thy name. — MATT. vi. 9.

NAMES have a deeper connection with things than we sometimes think. There was a time in the earlier ages of the life of the human family when the name of any object had a living interest attaching to it. It fitted naturally to that thing which it described. The same novelty and beauty which men saw in the universe into which the race was newly born to consciousness and knowledge of itself, sparkled and shone in the speech which described these transcendent wonders. Language has become common now. We use words as counters of convenience. Only when we pause and reflect upon it do we realize that the counters are of pure gold. The science of language, by tracing the mutations of human speech and the laws by which they are governed, has gone far with its students to restore to words their primitive freshness. But in our usual use they are still *rusted over* with commonness.

With the names of *persons* the case is very different. Here the instinct of individuality preserves the name as in some sort sacred. A man cannot change his name at will, to suit his own pleasure. He who forges the signature of another is a criminal in the eye of the law. The name is a part of the very self.

Thus we are led to understand the connection of *religion* with the words which are the expression of its mighty thoughts. What philology does for the phrase of our daily speech, what the strong instinct of individuality does for the personal name, — exactly that, only in a far more eminent degree, religion does for its own great words in the forms of language which it uses. It fills them out with their own true fulness of meaning.

The name of *sin* expresses the awful power of evil, involving unutterable suffering to those who fall beneath its dominion; the name of *soul* expresses all the vast, mysterious endowments which are wrapped up in our spiritual nature; the name of our Lord Jesus Christ expresses the power of his religion, the vital spiritual force which renders the truths of religion operative upon the human heart (as the great phrase of the fathers has it), the saving power of the gospel of Christ. You cannot separate these in your thought from him in whom the principles of Christianity were inseparably bound up. And the Supreme Name of all, the Awful Name of God, expresses the soul's idea of infinite power and wisdom and love, — all those attributes which inhere in our thought of the Ruler of the Universe, all-wise, all-powerful, all-holy, and all-good.

We can see, then, why it is that our Saviour, in teaching his disciples to pray, should make them ask, as their very first request, something connected with this Name, — that is to say, with this supreme thought of God. There are other things which are good for us, necessary for us, which, on our usual theory of what prayer is, we should begin by asking for.

What can we ask for more urgently than that without which we should starve, — the bread of each day, whose food we must have to keep us in the life of this body; the bread of the mind, whose sweet and wholesome thoughts we must have to nourish us; the bread of the heart, to sustain us with love and comfort us with the solace of dear companionships; the bread of the soul, to be ennobled by high, devout thoughts, and to feel that we are growing purer, better? This on one side of our need; and then yet deeper, more intense, the cry of the spirit, in its bitter sense of shortcoming and sinfulness, for pardon and reconciliation. Sooner than the very food without which we die, give me, — is the prayer of the soul, — give me some promise that I shall be lifted out of this slough of despond at my own weakness and wanderings from God; lift a light upon me which shall show me the way I can walk in, and roll off from me the burdens which hinder me therein.

Give me and *forgive me;* these two petitions are the substance of liturgies and prayers, — the natural asking of the soul when it passes out from the chambers of self-content and seeks to enter the presence of the All-Giver by the portal of prayer. And Christ recognizes by and by, a little later, in this great prayer of his, that these needs are true, that only God can satisfy them, that their cry to Him is right and fit. Only, he says, not yet, not yet. You must begin on a higher plane even than your own consciousness of your need, if you will save your need from degenerating into a self-absorbed and self-seeking cry. We can be selfish even in our prayers. How many Te Deums have been sung in great cathedrals for victory over one's enemies, in utter forgetfulness of this truth! How many Christian men have prayed in health and wealth long to live, and have really begun and ended all that was genuine in their prayers with that! How many have even besought forgiveness of their Maker, not so much from love to Him and desire to be in accord with His perfect law of righteousness, as from a sense of personal discomfort, and a desire to have it removed!

Think, therefore, first of all, our Master bids us, of that which is infinitely above yourself.

Fill your soul with the great thought of God. If you lift your soul to it, you will lift your soul's desires also to a point where they will be purged from selfishness, and their answer will be such as you can safely bear.

The duty of reverence in our thought of the eternal Name is no new duty, indeed, of Christianity. For if you should ask me what was the central truth of the ancient religion, — of the religion of the Hebrews, — I should answer, it was an awful reverence for God. That treasure it enshrined and has passed on to the Christian Church, with all the consecrating veneration of four thousand years, — from Abraham to Moses, from Moses again to Christ. Yet this great thought was not easily enrooted in the Hebrew mind; nor was it the common possession of good men and women, as it is to-day. As we look back through the centuries which went to the ripening of this consummate fruit of pious reverence in the souls of men, it is a *process*, long and slow, that we behold, — not the instant grasp of a great inspiring vision by a whole race. That which was revelation to a few — the morning sunlight touching the mountain summits, lofty souls that looked toward the day — was to the mass slow and painful teaching. They looked up to the glow of the morning on those heights whose pure snows were touched with "God's awful rose of dawn;" but they themselves were in the valley. Only so can you explain the repeated lapses of the Jews into idolatries, their golden calves and worship in groves and going after strange gods, accepting the sensuous rites of the nations round them, — Astarte, Moloch, and the rest. They had hardly learned the alphabet in which the name of the living God is spelled. And so the whole religion of the Hebrews, as we read it in our Old Testament, may be said to be one long schooling in the spelling of that Name. The Levitical law, with its ritual of external observances, all tends to teach this thought of sacredness through the sanctities of habit and usage which it impresses upon every detail of life on its religious side. The prophets burn and glow with this divine fire; the sacred law has it for its solemn undertone. The history shows us a people slowly struggling, with many a slipping back, toward that which it did not really attain till it had been ground to powder in the great Captivity, — the faith in God as their God. Yet all the time the ideal was there, summed up in the commandment, "Thou shalt not take the name of the Lord thy God in vain." Not only in the Law, but outside of the Law and beyond it, the Jews were taught to hold in veneration the word which represented God to them. They were not even allowed to speak it aloud when they read the sacred book. Their scribes could not write it, except with a pen which had not been used before. By and by another word would be substituted for it; or they could not write it at all in full, but only with a few letters of the word; and no one to-day certainly knows how that name which we spell *Jehovah* was pronounced.

All this belonged to the period after the Captivity, when, as I have said, the veneration for the sacred Name was deepening down into the hearts of the people, — formal, blind, and outward often, doubtless, but making the foundation-ground on which faith in that which the Name stands for could be built up.

1. The first thing, then, that we ask for in this petition is that this reverence which the Christian ages have ripened may be in ourselves,— that we may have a hallowed and hallowing sense of what that Name really means. It means much, unspeakably much, as we read it in the Bible, in that succession of names, each indicating a growing and greatening conception of the Divine character, and only partly made clear to the English reader, even in the Revised Version of the Old Testament. Far back in the beginning He is disclosed as Elohim, the creative powers which other peoples worshipped in scattered manifestations, brought to a focus, so to speak, in the one Creator. Then follows the patriarchal period, when men know Him as El Shaddai, the Almighty; and then the great revelation to Moses, "I am Jehovah; and I appeared unto Abraham, unto Isaac, and unto Jacob as God Almighty; but by my name Jehovah I was not known to them," — that

is, as the self-existent Being, the Living God. And then came Christ, showing us that this God is fatherly.

All these great names which we owe to our religion teach us sides of the Divine nature. Yet the full meaning of each must be disclosed by fresh light for each heart and soul freshly; and it would be atheism for us to say that He had exhausted all manifestations of Himself. "There is no word that is large enough to hold all the truth that God has told men about Himself."

He writes that Name in unsyllabled characters on the earth and on the sky, in the beauty and the blessing of this vast and radiant universe which He has made. He reveals Himself to the reverent eye in the great march of human history, and in the Providence which such an eye cannot but trace in countless lives. He speaks in that august life of power and help in which Jesus Christ, His well-beloved Son, has forever made His presence a fact not to be gainsaid or denied, — the incarnate Word of the God who is our Father, speaking to us in accents of grace and truth. And in that pleading Spirit which is God in living contact with the living soul of His child, he makes all things new for whomsoever will receive it.

We live in a universe that is full of the manifested God, for those who will see Him, — always full of His presence and His power; more and more clearly known through the disclosures all along the ages to saints and sages, who, as they travelled along the different paths of faith or knowledge or hope or love, have seen His light shining on their way. What prayer so well befits human beings in this overpowering Presence as the prayer, "Hallowed be thy Name"?

2. But that which ought to be the heart of our desire toward God is deeper and closer even than this attitude toward His disclosures of His great Name. It should be nothing less than that His Name might utter itself through us, through our own personal thought of Him, — the conception of His character which we make the motive power of our life. There is an eternal truth in that mysterious narrative in the book of

Genesis which describes Jacob wrestling with the unseen Power "until the breaking of the day." "And Jacob asked him, and said, Tell me, I pray thee, thy name. And he said, Wherefore is it that thou dost ask after my name? And he blessed him there."

"Come, O thou traveller unknown,
  Whom still I hold, but cannot see!
My company before is gone,
  And I am left alone with thee.
With thee all night I mean to stay,
And wrestle till the break of day.
            .   .   .   .   .
"Yield to me now, for I am weak,
  But confident in self-despair;
Speak to my heart, in blessings speak;
  Be conquered by my instant prayer.
Speak! or thou never hence shalt move,
And tell me if thy name be Love.

"My prayer hath power with God; the grace
  Unspeakable I now receive;
Through faith I see thee face to face,—
  I see thee face to face and live!
In vain I have not wept and strove;
Thy nature and thy name is Love."

It is the personal struggle for a noble, a living conception of God—for a name by which we can

Hallowed be Thy Name. 69

call Him with all the best allegiance of our own souls — which wins the blessing forevermore.

For we should not suffer ourselves to forget that what a man thinks, feels, believes about God is the deepest thought and faith in him. We all take the same name upon our lips; but there is an immense range in the real meaning and dignity and value of that name to different men and women. So it was that all the monstrous misgrowths and abominations of superstition arose in the beginning. Men believed in a God; there was that in their own souls which compelled them thereto. But what kind of a God? By what name should they call him? And they distorted "the light which lighteth every man that cometh into the world" by all manner of broken refractions, till they came to worship and cringe before that which was lowest and worst, and called that divine. Do you say that all this was long ago, — that Christianity has changed all this? Has it, then, changed it wholly? We have indeed discarded the ancient misbeliefs; but is there no danger in the opposite extreme, — that we will have but a very imperfect and powerless idea of God? Partial and incomplete must be the most perfect thought which we can have of Him, of course. Yet what a gulf is there between the thought of Him which some have, as relentless will, power working by law without love, on the one hand, or on the other, as a Being who has relaxed the austere bonds of the moral order of the universe, who does not care much whether His children do right or wrong, but will somehow save them from the consequences of their own misdoing, — what a gulf, I say, between either of these, and the pure and living and powerful thought of Him which is given to us in Jesus Christ, as our Father, who loveth and worketh righteousness!

It would be easy to show that everything which we have to-day which is of real worth in our modern life comes from men who have had this great, vital conception of God. They have not sat still in easy-going fashion, but have wrestled as Jacob did for a name great and worthy enough by which to call the Power that ruled their lives, and have won that blessing, and in winning it have won by their faith and self-sacrifice everything that our civilization gives us to-day.

And certainly, even though our highest thought of Him can but dimly state His perfectness, we must believe, if we look at it seriously, that it will make an immense difference to us in the way we live, in what we do, whether we think of God as highly and as holily as we can, or whether we fall short of that, — whether we hallow His Name.

We know, indeed, that it is quite beyond *our* power to hallow it worthily. To keep the thought of God, in all the height and depth of goodness and of greatness which are bound up in the ineffable Name, so enshrined in our souls that they shall always be possessed and overruled by it, — that our business shall not crowd it into the background, nor our weariness cause it to fade away into dimness, nor our sorrow darken its light, nor our temptations mar its peace, nor our doubts shake its certainty, — who of us is able? Who of us sinful men can keep that holy shrine in his soul for the holy God? It is just because *we* cannot, that we pray *God* to do it. The very inspiration of our religion is its teaching that the Living God is able and willing so to make the souls of His children His dwelling-place.

So, too, with what is really the other side of our petition,— with the question what we can do to help make His Name hallowed in the world. What *without* Him we cannot do at all, *with* Him we can do much to aid. The prayer that His Name may be hallowed really asks that the time may come when all men shall know Him and love Him as the best men now know and love Him. He answers such a prayer as that partly through His faithful children doing something to make Him more real in power and blessing to the trust and loyalty of other men. When that prayer is perfectly fulfilled it must be because *every one* of us, not in our own strength but in God's strength, has done something to persuade our brethren that this world is God's world, that they are His children.

Now, every life that makes clearer any scattered gleam of any one of those eternal qualities which are part of God's own nature, does thus spell out some letter or syllable of His Name for the acceptance of other hearts, who believe *that* because they *see* it. The poor African women who in their rude hut sheltered Mungo Park in his adventurous exploration (in that story so dear to the hearts of the boys of my generation), and gave him a mat to lie upon, and pounded corn for his supper, while they sang, "The white man has no mother to grind his corn," did more to make God's pity a living fact, though they only knew God by a dim natural instinct — can we doubt it? — than many a worshipper who bends the knee in a Christian church, yet with a heart bitter toward his fellow-men. The old Persians used to teach their children, as a religious duty, to speak the truth. Surely that fine sense of the fitness of truth, the shame and disgrace of falsehood, was a testimony to Him whose very name is truth, and who has made the unerring order of the universe to be true to the end of time. Take it in our own day. The engineer of the train wrecked in a collision, who rushes to sure destruction with his hand on the throttle of his engine, when he might escape by leaping from his post of duty, — why do you applaud instead of pitying him? Probe your judgment of the case to the last analysis, and you will find that you prize human faithfulness because it is in accord with the Divine fidelity, and testifies to Him one of whose noblest names is the Faithful God.

We read a day or two ago how last Wednesday night, while we slept in the safe shelter of our homes, a vessel bound for this port, coming from southern sun and warmth, was driven in the blinding snow-storm, at midnight, on Scituate beach. Perhaps you have stood there in some such wild fury of the elements, and watched the tremendous uproar of the waves pounding the solid shore as if they would drown the very continent, while the beacon-tower far out at sea tells only the little utmost that human power can do to warn of the peril, — the *nothing* that it can do to help. Was it because those brave hearts did not hold life dear, that men were there to launch the life-boat in those tumultuous waters, and to rescue the shipwrecked men from certain death in the horror of storm and cold and darkness? You are thrilled by their splendid courage, I say again, if you probe your feeling to the last analysis, because it testifies to the God who has made men worth saving, and has given them the power of self-sacrifice.

Now take all these great and heroic traits of human nature which do so much to make the Divine power which rules our human lives known and honored, and touch them with the last and supreme trait which is possible to the human soul, — a *conscious loyalty* to God as the Christian knows Him, as our Father. If He is *that*, His children ought to have something in them to show the likeness and to persuade men to live holier, sweeter, purer lives by seeing His glory reflected in these human faces that look up to His light. That was the way the world was made Christian in the beginning; men beheld in the first disciples the reflected divineness of that in the Lord Christ which showed the Father; and they rose and followed where that light led, into newness of life. It is so still. An Afghan once met

Dr. William Marsh, a saintly missionary, and remained an hour in company with him. The impression made by his character was so strong as never to be forgotten; and when afterward the Afghan learned of Dr. Marsh's death, he said, "His religion shall now be my religion, his God shall be my God; for I must go where he is and see his face again."

There can be few of us so poor as not to have had something like that come true in our own experience. The evidence of lives evidently childlike, possessed and made holy by the spirit of their Father, convinces us of *immortality*, because we are sure that He has looked on them and is well pleased; and "in His favor is life," — convinces us of *God*, because we are sure that the faith which is strong enough to carry such souls to victory cannot be a delusion.

Such lives are the putting into effect of this great and holy petition that His Name may be hallowed. It is for us to make it ours in the spirit of Christ: "Father, glorify Thy Name. Then, came there a voice from heaven, saying, I have both glorified it, and will glorify it again."

THY KINGDOM COME.

IV.

THY KINGDOM COME.

Thy kingdom come.—MATT. vi. 10.

WAS there ever a heart created so poor in ideals and hopes as never to desire that the world should improve; that things should go on (if they were despondent) from bad to good, or (if they were of cheerful temperament) from good to better? Was there ever one who did not feel, no matter how bright or masterful or conquering a life he succeeded in living, that it was quite beyond his own power to bring this future Golden Age to accomplishment, even with himself in any perfect degree, far more in any large way with the world.

The desire that a kingdom, a fairer realm than the present should come; the sense that it belongs to God and not to us,—these two forces converge in the petition in our Lord's Prayer, Thy kingdom come!

Yet there are more ways than one of praying it, more dispositions than one which may feel that the prayer encourages their mental attitude towards the world, filling it full of their own meaning instead of finding Christ's meaning — God's meaning — in this mighty prayer.

There are those — and their name is Legion in this active, generous, unselfish age of philanthropies and charities, of day-dreams of a millennium, or of earnest labors for the bettering of humanity — who look to see a multitude of wrongs set right. By wholesome teaching or restraining laws, a more enlightened self-interest or a more disinterested public spirit, they hope to see the prayer put into effect. Thy kingdom is not yet, they say. Evil men have thus far hindered it; let it come to the weary and struggling earth as the sun comes bringing morning out of night.

Others there are, and not seldom these very ones of whom I speak come to be such, for whom even this vision of a redeemed and renewed earth does not exhaust the desire of their souls. They have tried the disappointments and the disillusions of life, and they know full well that even if the poor vessel in which all these earth-bound hopes are contained — this globe itself — could be passed, so to speak, through these fiery, regenerating heats, which would make it over, porcelain instead of common clay, it would be brittle and hollow still, quite too perishable a vessel to imprison all the needs, and too small to contain the satisfaction of all the longings of the human soul. They have not greatly succeeded, and they know they never can, in this world; they have loved, and what they most care for has had its sunset out of their sky. The real desire of their souls is, "O that I were a dove; then would I fly away and be at rest," in a land very far off which they hope for, of light and joy and peace, the kingdom which is not of this world.

Yet there is a hope more spiritual than the first of these, and more hopeful and manly than the second. I may desire to see the world better than it is, and may believe that it can become so, yet not be satisfied with the mere bettering of its conditions on the earthly plane. I may feel that there is an enlargement which only God can give, yet not put it utterly beyond the horizon of the life that now is. "Some indeed would say," if I may quote Mr. Maurice, "that the source of this sense of beauty and righteousness and truth is *in* themselves; if men were but great and noble and free . . . they would perceive it. Others affirm that when they exalt themselves this secret is hidden from them; that they enter into it only when they are humbled. The first would say, not indeed in a prayer, but in their professions, their daily acts, their processes of self-discipline, '*My* kingdom come;' let my spirit be lightened of the outward impediments which prevent it from being right, wise, free; let it be lifted to its proper throne, from which it may look upon all beneath and around it, and if there be aught above it, as its own possession. The other says, 'Thy kingdom come;' let the eyes of my understanding be cleared of their native mists, that they may see thy wisdom; let me be purged of my inward pride and self-seeking, that I may know thy truth; let me be set free from my exceeding sinfulness, that I may confess thy righteousness and be clothed with it. And that this may come to pass, do thou take the government of all that is within me, of conscience, affection, reason, will, that they may do thy work and not their own."

And now if we turn to him who gave us this prayer, to Jesus, our Saviour, to know in which of these interpretations of it our souls shall find rest, he leaves us no room for doubt. It is the largest possible, and it touches all lesser interpretations with light and fulness.

The phrase "the kingdom of God," was, in the day of Christ, the natural expression on the lips of many of his countrymen of their dearest longing; but it was a very materialistic kingdom which they prayed for. They saw the hated foreigner exercising dominion over them; they believed that the Messiah's kingdom would be the rule of a prince of their own blood, a second David, over an independent nation, as God's vicegerent. Jesus took the hope which he found there, purified and transfigured it, and gave it as an eternal possession to mankind. He did not rebuke it or contradict it; he ennobled it, and so made it a hope great enough to answer all the unsatisfied longings of men's souls. The two classic passages which define the Christian conception of God's kingdom, out of a hundred or more in the New Testament which speak of it, are certain words of Christ and of Saint Paul. When some of the Pharisees asked Christ when the kingdom of God should come, his answer was, "The kingdom of God cometh not with observation; neither shall they say, Lo here! or Lo there! for, behold, the kingdom of God is within you." And his great apostle says, writing to the Romans, "For the kingdom of God is not meat and drink, but righteousness and peace and joy in the Holy Ghost." That is to say, the kingdom *is*, not merely shall be, by and by, here or hereafter. It is an interior, spiritual kingdom, and no outward, material improvements in civilization can exhaust its benefits for us. It is in those spiritual gifts which are in their very nature *powers;* and so it must be cumulative, — a richer treasure, a larger blessing, a fuller kingdom, all the time.

I think there is nothing which we so much need as this great and hopeful faith in the present, ruling God. The imperfections of this world, and of ourselves, are not difficult to perceive. The fact that this world is *in the making*, only, is plain enough to every one.

Men have always grasped, from the beginning, this great fact; religious men have laid hold upon it as giving a clue full of light and comfort to the darkest mysteries of this human life; and even those who could find no light or hope in it have felt its power, like the iron stroke of a flail beating on their hearts. The truth that the Almighty Maker of our lives and Father of our spirits has placed us here not as He might have done, doubtless, with finished and symmetrical lives, everything happy and smooth about us, everything bright and easy within us, characters complete and rounded, minds and hearts whose even pulse-beat kept temperate time, the voices of neighbors and friends making harmonious music on our way, the business of our calling running with untangled threads, no shadow of disease, no dread of loss, no agony of parting; but, instead, in a world overhung with mystery and filled with discipline, the machinery of life needing constantly to be oiled and tended, and even then getting out of running gear, the human relations of it so complicated, so difficult, hardest to do one's full duty in for those whose conscience in duty is keenest, our own selves the most unquiet kingdom for ourselves to rule, with puzzles of heart and will and brain and conscience, and over all the shadows which men knew of old as the visitings of Fate, and which, though they know them now as the touch of a merciful God, gathering the soul into the hollow of His hand, they still must see in part as what they are on their earthward side, — change and sickness and pain and loss. The only solution is the double truth: that God has not finished but is still *making His world;* and that He does not work in this *alone,* but calls for the co-operation of man and nature with Him.

I do not need to linger to tell you how all the study and modes of expression which belong specially to our time tend to emphasize these truths on the side of the natural order. Blank with denial only to those who will shut their eyes, radiant with the progressive unfoldings of the Divine Presence and Purpose, to the reverent vision and the consecrated heart, how could any new statement of the laws of Nature fail to be, for those who believe that all those laws are only the perfect working of the Perfect One? And the ever deepening sense that the world is one ought surely to bring us more and more to the faith that as He works in the universe without, so He is working in the universe within, the character, the life, the soul, with a steady unfolding of His purpose, a progressive recreation of that which He thought it well to make in the beginning, that He might remake it continually, from good to better, and from better to best.

And so, in very truth, we find it, when we really try with reverent and careful hand to unwrap the foldings which conceal from us the meaning of our human life, and to get at the heart of it. This is pre-eminently a case where the evidence is *cumulative*. It grows larger, more convincing for every religious mind, the more we look back upon our own past, — the broader the sweep with which we are able to embrace and take in great pieces of that past in one general survey. To the young Christian who knows little by personal knowledge of the things which make the burden and the weight of life, the cares, the disappointments, the failures, the sorrows, it must needs be that he takes them on faith; the doctrine of God's method in the life of men is of necessity to him a hearsay truth, and not one which he has learned at first hand. It is only when year after year has brought its lengthening evidence to him that there is a Power shaping his life beyond, and above, his wisest plans for himself, how its earthly thwartings have been Divine leadings, its desert ways have led by unexpected fountains of Divine water, and the very fragments into which its strong mountains have been broken have been as stones quarried for the walls of the New Jerusalem, — only then does the faith become an assured conviction.

We all would agree, I suppose, in a more or

less defined feeling that this principle holds good in such cases as these where it has to do with the working out of characters distinctly *religious*, and where it manifests itself in the graces which we recognize as *Christian* in form as well as substance, which, as Jeremy Taylor says, "take root downward in humility, and blossom upward in piety." But we can come far outside of that boundary line which we thus arbitrarily draw for ourselves, between the soul on its spiritual side and the same soul in its development of character, in relation to law and duty. This is, indeed, where our Christianity ought to help us, for it is exactly here that it is vitally distinguished from other modes of religion; it has a finer insight, and is armed with a more potent instrument for discerning the true scope of spiritual relations and the real breadth of the spiritual universe. It is somewhat like the process by which the spectrum of the sun's rays has recently been explored to a reach far beyond its supposed limits, and compelled to disclose mysteries of wonder where there seemed to be nothingness. A keener eye, if I may say so, was invented, which could pierce where human vision stopped baffled, — and lo, where it seemed to be pure darkness was full of the secrets of light! And so if we arm our moral and spiritual perception with the divine insight of Jesus Christ, we can see how the moral spectrum, so to speak, extends far beyond the limit which we might suppose, which multitudes of men have supposed, which great religious and historic faiths have been willing to admit. The unerring lines which tell the story of what it means, and of its unity in the Divine Plan, can be read in an unbroken sequence from the most intense brightness of the religious life as it shines with dazzling radiance and expresses itself most vividly in great saints and spiritual heroes, all the way through the shadowed silence in which reserved characters, dumb to articulate expressiveness, are yet manifesting the same law of light and truth.

Dr. Bartol says: "In a late French story, one of the characters is an atheistic surgeon in a hospital, where his niece, a young girl, is a devotee.

He performs the bloody operations, she carries round the ointment and lint. 'What,' she says to him one day, 'do you hope for after death?' 'Rien, rien, rien,' he replied. Afterward, as they make their circuit together, he informs her he has a fatal disease which he knows will shortly end his life, and asks if, on his sending for her, she will come to see him at the last. She assents. Soon his visits stop, and his message entreating her presence arrives. She finds the anteroom of his house filled with the poor, grateful patients he had gratuitously relieved, and his chamber door barred against the priest striving to enter in vain. She is admitted alone, and at once falls, — no, that is no human motion, — is thrown to her knees at the bedside of the dying man. 'O Lord,' she cries, 'bless him. Hast thou not declared that thou wouldst bless those that have fed the hungry, clothed the naked, visited the sick, and in prison? That is what he has been doing all his life. Now, Lord, fulfil thy promise and bless him.' The old man murmurs from his pillow, 'It is not necessary to overdo this. I have simply discharged my professional duties, nothing more.' A pause of silence between them ensues, interrupted by the expiring man: 'Pray again, my child, pray again. It is a music that pleases me.'"

Ah, friends, can there be any music so sweet as the awakened sense that one has done something by faithfulness and unselfishness to bring that kingdom nearer which "is not meat and drink, but righteousness and peace and joy in the Holy Ghost!" But it makes an immense difference in the "lift" and inspiration of our lives, whether our thought of it has the upward or the downward look, whether we believe in it as well as long for it.

Everything in which the world is moving forward from good to better, from better to best, is the coming of His kingdom on earth; every gain in spiritual life, in faith, in hope, in love, every enlargement of the possibilities of character, every opening of the windows of the soul, is that kingdom made more real in individual lives. It is *in progress*, not finished; and so we may well pray that it may come, and still that it may more fully come. It has *begun to be* here already; and so, above all else, we may well pray in hope, assured that it has already been answered and will be answered more and more.

This prayer means nothing less than that this whole human society of which we are a part may be transformed into the likeness of God, — till there is not a life here so stunted or so darkened or so defiled as not to be lifted into His light, and made sweet and clean and strong, — when "the kingdoms of this world shall become the kingdom of our God and of His Christ."

Is it not a noble vision? is it not an inspiring hope? is it not worth praying for, both with that yearning cry of our souls to God which will bring His answer, and with that strenuous bending of our lives to His service which is prayer making itself real in act?

We can see, then, how the different modes of looking at this thought of the coming of God's kingdom are all touched by Christ. It is to be a better world; a happier and a richer in all good things, a more wholesome home for His children to live in, — this world that now is; and that is a good gift, and it comes down from the Father of lights Himself. But that is not all. There is comfort here for the weary and heavy laden; the great hope which lays hold on the life immortal, which knows that no life would be worth living here on earth that was untouched by that mysterious and blessed light transfiguring all human sorrow and desolations; that no life would be life hereafter in which those whom God gave us here did not meet us again as His best gift to the reawakened spirit; this hope shall be fulfilled in that eternity which is God's and where He is and his children with Him. And the great desire of the soul for those best gifts, the thirst for goodness, truth, holiness, which can only be satisfied by the consciousness of being ruled by the Living God, — the very coming of Christ was an answer to the prayer; it made real for men forever the certainty of God's ruling care; it brought into full being that interior kingdom of the willing, loyal spirit, where God is enthroned.

"Thy kingdom come!" We pray that prayer often forgetting that it has been prayed before us, and to some purpose, for near two thousand years. It is a wonderful thought that, from the day when Christianity came to be at home in the world, men have been asking for this, and surely have not asked in vain. Even when their prayer seemed to be denied, we can look back now and see that it was answered in a higher, deeper way. The early disciples prayed it, and instead of the speedy reign of the Messiah, were dispersed over the whole earth. But the gospel went with them, as wind-wafted seed on the breath of a tempest. Our Puritan forefathers prayed it in England, and persecution smote them and drove them forth, homeless fugitives. But they were "the sifted wheat of the three kingdoms," and this America is a diviner answer to their prayer than they could have dreamed. But whether answered in the fashion than it seemed to ask, or otherwise, the whole progress of human history is an illuminated commentary upon it for hundreds of years, and not alone within the pale of our religion but outside of it, wherever He hath not left Himself without a witness. For there cannot be any gleam of pity, any sense of tenderness, any light of faith in goodness or awe and trust, from the earliest prayer of the savage to the sublime surrender and joy of the Christian saint, in which God has not been coming to His children. And we, who are in the line of the Christian ages, as we look back through sixty generations who have prayed "Thy kingdom come," sometimes despondently and sometimes jubilantly, we ought to hear the answer as it has been given from generation to generation, as freedom has come, and knowledge, the loosening of fetters from the body and the mind and the soul of men.

Is there any prayer which comes, or ought to come, closer into our own lives than this? We pray it every one of us here in the church, and they who do not pray it elsewhere are poor indeed. What are we going to *do* about it? Will you try to help answer it? For even our God could not bring it to pass against the resistance of our human wills.

Can we pray "Thy kingdom come," and then go and thwart it by meanness in our business, by churlishness in our prosperity, by bitter tempers in our homes, by undevoutness in our religion, by impatience in our sorrows, by ungentle and unloving lives?

Shall we not rather put ourselves in the current in which the ages run, and all good and true lives move, and where the help and strength which never fail those who trust in them are given, and say to our own souls, "Lift up your heads, O ye gates, and be ye lifted up, ye everlasting doors, and the King of Glory shall come in"?

THY WILL BE DONE.

V.

THY WILL BE DONE.

Thy will be done, as in heaven, so in earth. — LUKE xi. 2.

THAT which every one likes best is to be able to say *I will*, — to exercise in our own place and degree a sort of lesser omnipotence, and to utter our *fiat* over creation, the little world of our own. *Fiat voluntas mea!* Most of us start in the beginning with a more or less clearly defined theory of this sort. And yet a very slight experience of life teaches us that if every one should act on this principle we should have unhappy times, — that just as far as the world has gone on that principle of pure and unmixed selfishness "chaos has come again." Here are a multitude of human wills, imperfect, selfish, conflicting; it is clearly impossible for any of us to have our own way to any considerable extent. And further, around, beyond, above, beneath this little world of human lives is a tremendous universe of elements and forces, in which this world is as it were an atom floating in infinite space.

So it is that even those who pray it least hopefully, or those who are not even hopeful enough to pray it at all, see as plainly as any one how great is the need that a higher will, an omnipotent will, — the will of God, — should control ours, and not ours only, but the whole universe. *Fiat voluntas tua!*

"Thy will be done." Probably no words in the whole Bible are so often on the lips and in the heart at the times when it really prays, as these. There are none which contain such a divine breathing of comfort for souls bruised by the storms of life, or smitten by its sorrows. They breathe, too, a trumpet-note, strenuous, inspiring, with a call to loftiest endeavor and a promise of undoubted victory; nor are there any words which embody such strength for the brave spirits who are working for the triumph of truth and justice, or who are struggling in manly fashion against adverse fates and winning the victor's crown, even though it be, as it not seldom is, by the martyr's cross.

Our Saviour well knew that the heart of humanity needed such a prayer, — that we needed above all things else to be able to see the hand of God in the events of life, so unexpected, so irresistible, and to trace them all, though through labyrinthine windings, to a love and mercy we could trust; yea, that we needed supremely to lose our own poor will, with its almost purposeless attempts, its fickle wanderings, its uncertain and irregular strivings after goodness, in the blessed consciousness of that Divine will, perfect though inscrutable, — which just because it is inscrutable we are constrained to believe is therefore perfect, — which shapes all these motions of its child's spirit into some harmonious fulfilment of the Divine purpose; that Divine will, which to have faith in fills the breast with light and peace. And because he knew this well, Jesus taught his disciples to pray in these words, which are the essence of Christian trust, and which indeed are the essence of all prayer, if we interpret them in their Christian breadth *actively* as well as *passively*. But although we use them so much, — perhaps, indeed, *because* we use them so much, — there is danger of our missing their full meaning.

When he who knew as no other the full meaning in which God is the Ruler, and His will the law of all things, gave us this petition, he did not by any means mean merely to repeat those words which had just gone before, — "Thy name be hallowed. Thy kingdom come." Rather does this prayer that His will may be done complete the rest. The *name* is God in Himself; "the *will* imports energy going forth." God being such an one as He is, infinite holiness, infinite love, His purposes must be pure blessing.

Again, when we ask for the coming of *His kingdom*, there is a wider compass in our prayer; we take in the whole world in our thought. But now we draw nearer to *ourselves*. We try to bring that power into our lives as it bears upon those lives. "Thy will be done." It is not mere *omnipotence* to which we pray. A being without the moral attributes of Christianity might be *that*, but the will would be one to dread. It is is far more than power that we worship; it is the God and Father of our Lord Jesus Christ.

We need, then, to beware first of all of a *fatalistic* way of viewing the connection of Providence with our earthly lives. There are certain black moods of the mind which are most likely to come upon us when some untoward thing has thwarted the direction of our lives, — a well-devised plan brought to nothing, a cherished hope crushed; or when all the powers of evil seem to encamp around the soul like savages in the woods around a frontier fort, and to be gradually but surely overcoming its resistance to temptation. Then we may easily find ourselves, weary and sick at heart, looking on the world as a great machine with most complicated mechanism, driven by the mighty engine of a relentless destiny, that seems to be shutting us up continually within narrower limits. In such a mood we fold the hands with a feeling of despair; and though we say, "Thy will be done," the voice within us seems rather to murmur, with the writer of Ecclesiastes, " Time and chance happeneth to them all."

Yet I hardly need argue that this is a feeling which we ought to resist with all the strength of our souls, — morbid and weakening, if we yield to it till it becomes the habitual state of the mind. Our forefathers spent much strength in discussing the problem of free will and predestination, — God's foreknowledge and determining purpose and man's ability. Our generation is more practical, — perhaps too little given to speculation on these high themes; and I suppose it would be impossible to-day to find a Christian congregation which did not practically accept both sides of the problem as equally facts, and which did not leave the whole matter there. But while we thus theoretically accept both, we are by no means free, in our actual conduct of life, from the danger of yielding to a practical fatalism which thinks it religious to leave all to God exactly in those matters where God and man must work together. He utters the Lord's Prayer with no true comprehension of its meaning who makes it an excuse to himself for supineness, and sits lazily by as the various events of life rush swiftly past him, doing no more to direct their course than the man who lives beside a rushing stream can do to control it when the rains have descended and the floods have come.

"Thy will be done!" we say. But that it may be done on earth, our hands and our hearts are needed.

The candle of a misspent and wasted life goes out in darkness; has God's will been done if *we* might have done something, and have failed to do our part, to shelter it from the gusts of passion which it was too weak and flickering in moral purpose to be able to resist?

Some great public wrong goes by default, and *we* might at least have prevented it from going by default, lifting a voice, even though it were but a solitary voice, in protest; can this miserable conspiracy of universal silence be the fulfilment of His will which is above all things searching, active, powerful?

And when we look within our own souls do not reason and faith and plain *common sense* (which, when touched with religion, is reason transfigured by faith), — do they not all revolt at the idea that we can forget to repent and reform, and then, forsooth, think it enough to accept the consequences of our own faults (which we ought never to have committed), and attribute it to the mysterious will of God, whose holy will really was that we never should commit them at all? No! we never were taught to say, "Thy will be done," merely as an easy way of shifting our own responsibility upon Heaven; but in order that we might, as the Apostle says, "gird up the loins of our mind" to perform every duty religiously, and thus make ourselves the instruments of God in the doing of His holy and acceptable and perfect will.

There is a less religious form of the same fatalistic temper which we have been speaking of. A great many persons say by the habit of their mind, We will leave the small affairs, the lesser matters of life, to take care of themselves; but when the great occasions come, those decisive moments which call for the quick eye and the swift purpose, we will find a worthy opportunity for honesty and courage and generosity. We can be mean, cruel, unfaithful, in all the petty relations of human beings with one another in which we are constantly involved. These have no binding hold upon us, to chain us in a leash of responsibility. Our duty will only be exigent in some rare moment; and then we cannot help doing it when we see it. Grant, for an instant, that this is so, and you are as strong as you think you are. The question at once arises, How are you to know the golden moment when it comes? Do you expect the will of your God to stand before you transfigured, as an angel? The eyes that are bleared with closely gazing on our own self-interest will hardly be able with their short-sighted vision to distinguish the majesty of this great opportunity which you have seen in your dreams with a halo. I suppose that even those whom the religious painters represent with a shining aureole about their heads walked this dusty earth as common men and women, and the careless passer saw in Peter or Paul only a fisherman casting his nets and a tent-maker plying his needle.

Or the very nearness of the opportunity will deceive you, and you will not realize how much it means. A mountain, when one stands at its base, dwarfs itself and seems no larger than the neighboring foot-hills. Or, once more, this occasion for doing some great thing may be very small in itself, made significant only by standing just in that place in the chain of similar events. As I rode with my friends in the far western part of Montana, through the heart of the Rocky Mountains, we paused to drink of a brook that gurgled across the high, broken plain, so level that it was impossible to realize that it was the dividing ridge of the continent. The rill was like any other; yet as the waters of the little stream parted at the spot where we stood, flowing toward the east and toward the west, they diverged never to meet again. You could turn the water in either direction by dropping a pebble in it, by putting your hand across it. But once turned it would never cease its course until it joined the Mississippi and flowed to the Gulf of Mexico, or till it was merged with the waters of the Columbia in the Pacific Ocean.

Or, suppose we know the opportunity when it comes; shall we be better fitted for it then, because we have *not* been preparing for it now? Does the neglect of small duties prepare us to perform great ones? The man who thinks that his arm will be developed of itself to the muscular power which can perform feats of strength, while it lies idle without lifting a finger in the hundred petty occasions of every day, will find it nerveless when the supreme moment of trial comes. Why should we expect any more that the moral and spiritual strength which we need in the exigent moments of our trial or our duty will come of itself, or be acquired without steady exercise?

No. It is very plain that the prayer, "Thy will be done," is only uttered in its true spirit when neither the mistaken theory that the omnipotence of God dwarfs man to impotence, nor the careless neglect of small duties as being of no account, prevents us from trying loyally to do our part in bringing to pass that perfect will "on earth," in the little planet which we rule, "as it is done in heaven," in the vast sweep of the Divine government through the countless ranges, height beyond height, which are above our human reach or knowledge.

But can we, then, learn what this will is? For obviously, if we cannot, *doing* it with any free, active, intelligent service would be impossible; and even *bearing* it would be but a grim setting the face as a flint against pitiless destiny. And surely here only those would doubt that in the Bible we can come deep and far into the purposes of God for His children who have not made acquaintance with that exhaustless fountain. Whatever else men have drawn out of it, — doctrine, controversy, theory, — however they have made it an armory of texts, they have never gone to it for a practical and practicable rule of life without finding there what they sought. Even the ancient Scriptures of the Old Testament are so saturated with the presence of a God of Righteousness, leading and teaching His children, that though the religion is progressive, and therefore in its earlier degrees imperfect, it points forward, so that even that strange old custom of opening its pages at hazard for a guiding word was likelier to give help than the modern way of leaving it unturned at all.

But we are not left to the Old Testament, we have the word of Christ; we have those writings of his first disciples on which the new world of Christian faith and trust was framed together. If any man wants to find a bridge with which he can span the mighty gulf which parts the seen from the unseen, — this human life from the great will of God, — let him try it with some sentence from the Sermon on the Mount, as one of the Beatitudes, or with some strong saying of Saint Paul; let him honestly try to build his life on that. He will find that he can trust his life safely to it.

"What are your marching orders, sir?" said the Duke of Wellington to a clergyman who was discussing a point of duty with him. "What are your marching orders?"

The old soldier's instinct was a sound one. Here is the Book which records how saints and heroes have been led on to victory, which gives their rule of life and the secret of their power, and shows the dangers of the way and sounds with their note of triumph.

Nor here alone is His will shown to us, but in all right and good things. What else are the voices of conscience, the call of duty, the joy of self-sacrifice, the blessing found in service? What else is the law written in light on all creation, and shining luminous in all true, faithful lives? The will of God! We must be blind if we cannot see it in all these, — a will which is *done*, not simply *borne*, and which can be done actively, gladly, trustfully. There is nothing, then, that a man does, which is a fit occupation for a human being to be engaged in at all, in which this prayer may not act itself out in the life.

Here is a lawyer, we will say. Has *he* a right to keep his desire that the will of God may prevail for Sundays, or for the time when some great trouble comes upon him? Are there not a hundred ways, quite within the scope of his regular professional duties, in which he can put it into effect if he will? Is the Golden Rule anything else than that prayer applied to the living of human beings in the same world together? Any of us who have been so fortunate as to know in a country town some wise, just lawyer of the old school, could tell very well — and the opportunity is not less large, perhaps, though not wholly the same, in our complex city life — how many occasions there are in which such an one can reconcile instead of fomenting discord; when he can advise to mercy instead of the pitiless exaction of claims which crush the poor; when he can carry through justice to its victory and prevent the triumph of the brazen offender.

Here is a business man; has it no concern *in* his business? His object is to make a fortune. Be it so. But the pursuit of this in all earnest, honest, honorable ways, is not incompatible with many ways of serving God as he goes along. For every man exerts an influence on society, of whose extent, perhaps, he little dreams. He will never know in this world how a petty meanness (for we do not speak here of acts absolutely dishonest) will give his neighbor courage to go one step beyond him. A man may even be unaware himself if his influence is a debasing one; just as he may breathe the atmosphere of a close room over and over again till it is heavy with the poison of the carbonic acid which he has breathed out, and yet himself hardly be conscious that its life is exhausted. So he may take away from the moral atmosphere all its vitality, filling it instead with impurities which insensibly stifle the moral sense and weaken the will and make drowsy the conscience of all who come within his sphere.

Or he may be high-minded, bringing the honor of chivalry into his business, scorning an unfair advantage of the ignorance of others, full of the charities which sweeten life, and transfiguring every action by a pure heart, a good conscience, and faith unfeigned; and the influence of a spirit so radiant and inspiring will penetrate like light, — as a sunbeam strikes through a dusty room and makes its path only brighter by the very motes that float in the air.

Here is your home! What is it if the spirit

of this prayer is forgotten? I know nothing sadder than the sight of parents without any defined principle of religious loyalty, living from day to day as if their children had no future, and there was no need of making them feel the reality of God's presence or of training them as immortal beings for the life beyond this life,— as if Christ had never been here and touched every soul with an eternal glory. Here are children with dormant powers of holiness and goodness, needing only the warmth of a sympathetic religious atmosphere to quicken their best nature into life. But the precious moments pass ungarnered. And then, when it is too late, and the character is set into its fixed mould, — hardened, it may be, against entreaty or example, — too often it is regarded by those who had these momentous responsibilities as part of the plan of Providence, something to bow before in submission as the inscrutable will of God.

When we look thus into the depths of God's holy will through this prayer, we find that its attitude is not of resignation only, but of the eager human will asking to find its happiness in doing something with God and for God. The great vineyard in which the Master calls us all to labor is seen to be no far-off vision on the sunny slopes of Palestine, made beautiful by the misty haze of distance, to be dreamed about by idlers in the market-place, but to lie at our very feet and to furnish work enough for our hand. I can easily see how such a consciousness of being a fellow-worker with God ought to raise a man to a higher level of spiritual feeling. It would touch his business and his home with a certain strong and tender light, in which conscience and love would be blended. His soul would be, as it were, a perfect glass to focus the rays of the Divine will as they shine through the clear atmosphere of a human spirit in harmony with its Father's Spirit; it would make them shine with kindly warmth on the poor, the desolate, because they first penetrated the inmost places of that soul itself with radiancy.

I thank God that I have been privileged to know not a few such souls, truly and bravely

Christian, whose whole life was a continual progress in goodness and holiness, — manly, womanly, with large natures, thoroughly human, lovable and beautiful on all the sides which we touch on the common levels, but rising to heights of character and going down to depths of trust which makes them moral and spiritual *powers;* not always endowed with remarkable gifts of genius or of culture, but simply earnest and faithful, evidently mastered and swayed by a profound allegiance to God: —

> "Thrice blest whose lives are faithful prayers,
> Whose loves in higher love endure.
> What souls possess themselves so pure ?
> Or is there blessedness like theirs ?"

We know well the other side of this prayer, the side which speaks with blanched lips of resignation and submission. Yet because men pray thus when they are powerless to avert what is sent to them, because every human heart must experience that sense of solitude and suffering, it would be a grievous mistake for us to think of this only as the *passive side* of this great prayer. No human being can submit in the uttermost stress of life's great calamities without using all the forces which God has put into our souls, and all the help which it can draw from His deep succors. When the soul tastes the bitter cup which was pressed to the lips of Christ in Gethsemane, we need to know that it is not only God's will, but His loving will. You have come beyond the sphere of any active doing of your own; you lie entirely in God's great hand; the spirit of resignation is plainly your necessity if you would have peace, your duty if you are a child of God. And where our necessity is also our duty it is plain that no mere passivity will serve our turn. A mighty resolve must be at the heart of our prayer, — the resolve to climb toward the light.

So comes the compensation. For as in a mountain valley where the winter's snow remains longest on the ground rare flowers blossom, which cannot bear the warmer soil of a more genial climate, so in those high hidden solitudes to which the soul struggles up amid the Alpine loneliness where it is in the secret chambers of the Most High, it finds "celestial blooms" which wither in the sunshine of a softer, brighter world. There is a heavenly-mindedness which it is hard to make a part of the very fibre of the soul, unless we have sought in the Lord's high places His peace that passeth understanding. There is a faith which is ripened by trial and pain, and makes us see through the mystery one thing at least in the darkness, — the great hand of God leading the soul from earth to heaven.

Many are those solitudes of the human soul. Hardest is it when it is the disappointment which comes through folly and sin. There is a point, even there, where those who are closest bound by ties of kindred or affection have done what they can, and can do no more. What shall we say when the mother sees her son sinking in the mire which his own sinful feet have trampled, wounding, all unregardful, the tenderest feelings of the hearts that love and can do nothing? It is not weakness, but the divinest fortitude which teaches such a spirit to say, "Thy will be done," and in trusting that inscrutable wisdom to find some balm for its mortal aches.

Or when all is gone but the precious memories which fill the past with light, and the priceless hopes whose light never goes down, it is not a weak sinking of the soul, but the strongest powers of our nature upborne and filled by the Spirit of God, which make confidence in the Divine mercy, and gratitude for all that has been, and faith in all that shall be, rise within the soul and silence the murmurs of the troubled stream of life against its stony bed, as the rising tide of the ocean stills the noisy waters of each creek and inlet which it fills.

There is room enough for submission, then, in the world, and in this prayer. Yet you cannot have even submission without something more; and in the prayer "Thy will be done" there is always a call to help in doing it, and a faith that it will surely be perfectly done at last, since it is the will of One who cannot fail.

"As in heaven so in earth," it says. And all the shining order of the sublime procession of obedience with which the stars in their orbits, and the company of angels and archangels and saints and holy ones go, as we believe, singing on their way to fulfil His tasks, bids us believe that we can do something to make this earth a heaven.

OUR DAILY BREAD.

VI.

OUR DAILY BREAD.

Give us this day our daily bread. — MATT. vi. 11.

WE have felt, I think, as we have gone on together meditating on the successive clauses of our Lord's great prayer that it was more full of teaching, of *doctrine* in the true meaning of the word, than we had supposed. And now as we come to the first petition which touches our personal wants, there is a lesson for us in the very place which this link holds in this golden chain which binds His asking children to the throne of God. This is the first word in which we speak of our own needs. We have approached our God not merely in the attitude of suppliants before an omnipotent Monarch, but as children coming to their Father; we have prayed that His Name may be hallowed; that men may know Him in His perfect attributes and may worthily honor Him; that His kingdom, which is over all, may more and more prevail; that His perfect will may be *done*, not simply *borne*, with free, willing service, everywhere as it is by the blessed ones in heaven. All this has taken you away from yourself, if you have really prayed it; it has filled the universe for you with God, nay, has not filled it, but has opened your eyes to see His fulness in it, who filleth all things. It seems as if Christ said to us, Wait, before you venture to ask for *yourself*. At the threshold of the Temple, lay aside all selfish thoughts, and try to make your own soul a living temple; when you have done that, you can trust yourself to approach the altar and ask your gift from it.

In a sermon from this text, preached on the first Sunday of Lent, Mr. Maurice has dwelt on the thought that in the Gospel which we shall read next Sunday our Saviour gives us a commentary upon this petition. The tempter said to Jesus, "If thou be the Son of God, command that these stones be made bread." He answered, "It is written, Man shall not live by bread alone, but by every word that proceedeth out of the mouth of God." That is to say, the one supreme need in regard to these matters which seem most *un*divine, the common things of our daily need, is that we should have the habit of dependence and faith. It is the truth which was symbolized by the pot of manna laid up in the ark of the Holy of Holies, a memorial of God's feeding His people in the Israelite wandering. And in the life of our Master this truth shines bright.

It is the lesson which ought to be the central thought of those commemorative forty days of Lent. So far as it is not a mere formal matter, so far as it is made a period of spiritual quietness and the gathering up of the soul's forces for renewal in religious strength, every soul must be the better for pausing to confront the great thought till we can make it wholly ours, that the things which most seem *ours* are primarily not *ours*, but God's, and ours by His grace. "Give us this day our daily bread."

Are we then to pray for material gifts? So it would appear, if we are to hearken to Christ. And if for *bread*, that is, the common things which we require to keep body and soul together, then for how many of the needs of body and spirit which widen out from that elemental point! Suppose for a moment that he had left these things altogether out of the account in summing up the things that we could rightly pray for, would you not feel that it was less well thus to lose the Christian consecration on the whole material side of life, that you could *not* pray for the things without which you could not live this earthly life at all, that when you draw near to God, you must leave them outside your thought of Him, outside the thought of His Power or His Care ? However you might be able to do this in the hour of your speculative questioning on this matter, you could not do it in the times when the deep places of your spirit were broken up, when you felt that you were compassed about with awe and mystery, and the finger of God touched you.

My friends, the deep need of man is the best interpreter of the deep purposes of God. The cry that comes out of the heart of the nature which He has made testifies truly to the heart of His own nature; it testifies that it is not a cry into dark emptiness, but into the darkness where God is, the answering God.

As we proceed farther and farther into the depth of this prayer, it seems to me that each sentence speaks more and more directly to the special need of our time. Our modern world is divided by the sharp exigencies of its earnest competitions, its keen business rivalries, the hurry and drive and fever of our life, into two opposite classes of people, — those who overwork, and those who do not work at all, or as little as they can; those who carry their own burdens and everybody's else, and those who are carried. Both need to draw near to Christ, to learn how the habit of their life, the desire of their souls, should be related to God. Stop long enough, the Master says to the man who wakes to a new crowded day of business care, and hastens from his home with hardly a greeting to his family, and with no leisure for a morning blessing on the day, — stop long enough to think that God is the Giver of all, the Source of the opportunity that waits for you to seize it, of the trained powers and gifts (we call them so) which you will put forth to get your gains, and so the free, lavish Giver to you American of this nineteenth century of those very things which it is the fashion of our nation and our age to plume ourselves upon as most distinctly *our own*. The time must come to every one of us when we shall know that nothing is *our own*, and that we hang on the great hand of God for the ebbing pulses of this life itself. Surely it will be well if we will anticipate a little that attitude of humility and waiting on our unseen Helper. We shall be less likely to be grasping and greedy, more inclined to be just, and generous too, if we keep this thought of the overflowing treasury of God's free benefits for us before our minds, thinking not so much of the sternness of His laws and the rigor of His demands upon us, as of His goodness and His grace. This on the one side; and on the other, for the lazy and the do-little members of the social order, there is a bracing tonic in this very petition of dependence. "Give us," we say; but how does He give? Not by the falling of the bread upon us through the air, but through the long process of sowing and reaping, nature and man working together, the grain which was a few scattered seeds is harvested at last; and then again follow yet other processes in which man's labor and the laws of chemical action work together. So, however your bread comes to you, you have no right to ask that it shall come without your working for it. God gives it to you by giving you a chance to get it, faculties that you can train to labor, a place in this world that you can find waiting for you to fill it, plenty of opportunity for hardness and persistency and fidelity. And so the ancient curse in the garden of Eden in the beginning, " In the sweat of thy brow shalt thou eat bread," is turned to blessing in the new life of Christendom.

But the prayer is only *for this day*. Again, how strange a contrast to the temper of our anxious, foreboding way of life, which is continually borrowing from to-morrow care to cloud the happiest present! Are we to say, then, that Christ really taught that we were to live as if there were no morrow, with spendthrift lavishness beggaring our future, or with indolent acquiescence leaving it unguarded? Did he mean that we were *so* to consider the fowls of the air and the lilies of the field? The question is its own answer. We interpret Christ by Christ; and in the spirit of his religion, and in other words of his, we find the meaning, and in our own lives abundantly the *wisdom* of his warnings against that feverish worry and strain, that rush after wealth at any price, those discontents and repinings which spoil the sweetness and mar the peace of so many. There are few of us who would not be helped if they could be met to-morrow in their hurry down town by one who would say to them, "A little more *living by the day* in the wise quiet of a sober mind would not hurt you, my friend. Try, for to-day, to possess your soul in patience. You have *this day* to live in. Put all the *life* into it you can, of goodness and love and trust."

"Give us this day our daily bread." I suppose there is no single sentence in the Bible or in all literature more in contrast with the average habit of mind of the average man of our time. Daily bread! is that what he is striving for, slaving for, wearing out his life to get? It does not in any wise follow that it would not do him good to try honestly to tone down his desires to this bounded limit. One thing is certain, — the richest man in America really gets for his wages only his food and clothes and a roof over his head. If he wins real respect, it is because his character justifies it; if he has intellectual tastes or pleasures to enrich his life, his money does not buy them. And if we would school ourselves to ask for *daily bread*, meaning a more sober limit on our hot ambitions, our race after money, our temptations to luxurious life, we should bring whole new horizons of light into our spirits.

Yes! bread is a plain word, but a wholesome one. A little more of that plainness in our thought and our desire would help to scatter the phantoms of social discontent which lower in our sky, — all the brood which hover like pestilential vapors over the fertile plain of this modern world. Not that Christ means to reduce the world to one level, and discourage provision for the future. Whatever you receive more than your daily bread is so much super-added. The more there is, the more duty does it bring with it to the mind which is touched by his light. More than we need is much; if you have it, use it as a faithful steward. But what we need is soon said, though it is nevertheless a great gift, — our daily bread. Having this, says an apostle, "let us be therewith content."

FORGIVENESS.—THE DIVINE SIDE.

VII.

I. FORGIVENESS. — THE DIVINE SIDE.

And forgive us our debts, as we forgive our debtors. —
MATT. vi. 12.

WE should agree, I suppose, with Mr. Maurice, that we should be sorry to lose the word "trespasses" which we use in our ordinary repetition of the Lord's Prayer. And yet another great teacher of our time is surely right when in his "Letters to the Clergy on the Lord's Prayer and the Church," he says: —

"There is one very simple lesson, needed especially by people in circumstances of happy life, which I have never heard fully enforced from the pulpit, and which is usually the more lost sight of, because the fine and inaccurate word 'trespasses' is so often used instead of the simple and accurate one 'debts.' Among people well educated and happily circumstanced, it may easily chance that long periods of their lives pass without any such conscious sin as could, on any discovery or memory of it, make them cry out, in truth and in pain, 'I have sinned against the Lord.' But scarcely an hour of their happy days can pass over them without leaving, were their hearts open, some evidence written there that they have 'left undone the things that they ought to have done,' and giving them bitterer and heavier cause to cry and cry again, forever, in the pure words of their Master's prayer, 'Dimitte nobis *debita* nostra.'"

The nature and the needs of man seem in many ways to be contradicted by external nature, and so here.

There is no forgiveness in the laws of nature. Immutable and pitiless, they work on with an unsympathizing perfectness of which the most faultless piece of human machinery is but a blundering imitation. No ignorance or innocence of the child prevents the fire from burning his hand when thrust into it. The avalanche feels the thrill of the traveller's cautious step stirring the slumbering snows on the upper Alps, and hurls its ruin down upon him. The winds and waters do not forgive the sailor who comes on a lee shore in a raging northeaster, but freeze him with the bitter ice that stiffens the shrouds, and rush at him with the white-tusked billows, and smite him against the cruel rocks. The laws of chemistry and physics are as sure as the mathematics; and acids never turn to alkalies, nor do projectiles drop half-way from the gun, for our convenience. The laws of nature never forgive.

What is history, but the proof of the unforgiving sequence of cause and effect?

Hence arose the idea of *Fate*. Men felt the iron laws constraining them, deaf to their cries, ordaining their lot of loss and pain, crushing them, while still the sunshine laughed and the skies were blue above them and Nature disregarded their calamity though their hearts should break. The austere and antique genius of Michael Angelo has caught the spirit of the old fable, in his picture of the Parcæ, where the three withered crones who spin and sever the thread of human life, sit in aged majesty of mien, and look forth from the canvas with stony, unsympathizing eyes on the humanity whose destinies they shape, but do not share. Fate was something higher and more powerful than the gods of Olympus, a dread power behind that of Jove himself.

And the sombre imagination of our Norse ancestors expressed the same thought in the myth that Odin himself must die at length, and his stormy Valhalla sink into the night of a Destiny darkening over all. And this Destiny was unforgiving. No prayers could change, no sufferings soften it. Its penalties must be "paid to the uttermost farthing."

And yet, side by side with an iron fatalism has gasped for life the human sense of *need*. Men have felt the need of forgiveness, and their longing has cried out even to the heavens which they believed deaf, in all manner of uttered and inarticulate petitions. Their sins and their sorrows were stronger than all their theories of *destiny;* and, as so often, the warmth of the heart has melted the icy logic of the head.

It is therefore one of the most interesting of all questions which concern the relations between man and God, — what the nature of Divine forgiveness is, and how we are to believe in it. There are three ways, and only three, of answering the question; two of them in one form or other as old as the questioning mind itself, and the other the Christian solution.

1. The first is that which we have already spoken of as drawn from the observation of the material facts of things. It says simply, "There is no such thing as forgiveness, at all. It is all a dream of human nature, which is always desiring the impossible and striving to reach the unattainable."

It turns its telescope to the furthest depths of the celestial spaces, and finds there only order and law; it peers with microscope into the finest dust of matter, and can discern no forgiveness there; and so far as it can read the laws of human nature and human society, it sees only cause and effect at work, — the cause unattainable, the effect unchangeable. And so it bids us cease our useless efforts to change the course of our fates; the only worthy prayer is a life conformed to the laws, the only escape from the penalties is to bear them. This view has great strength in our experimental age, the strength of harmony with the new facts which are fascinating us all, and which seem almost to lift the curtain from the hidden secrets of creation, the strength of consistency with itself, and of the simplicity which seems to explain everything by grasping the central thought of all. But it is as weak as it is strong; for it is liable to the criticism that it breaks its own law, and theorizes beyond the legitimate proof of its facts. Its facts are *material; God* is *spiritual;* and it is incompetent to interpret spirit by matter. Its facts are partial, because they do not cover the whole domain of fact, and leave out of cognizance the facts of the human soul, whose longings and prayers are just as real as a fossil in the stone or a planet in its orbit. And it is difficult to see wherein the fatalism of a theory which eliminates a free God from His universe and from all connection with His children is the gainer over the most rigid fatalism of the Calvinism which puts men in the chains of predestination and foreordination. That at least preserves for men the living will of a personal God, and a chance that some of them may find a pitying ear in their prayers.

2. And yet the *arbitrary* theory of forgiveness contains dreadful inconsistencies. This is the idea of a school of theology which has had great and most hurtful influence in Christian teaching. By a most unjust misinterpretation of the *letter* of Saint Paul's epistles, the noble apostle has been made out the main pillar in a horrid system which is as foreign to the gospel of free grace which he offers as to his own royal nature. But the words of *Jesus* can never be even *forced* into a support for this theology, which combines the logic of the head with the atheism of the heart. The essential thing in it is the sovereignty of God. As if God could ever be so sovereign as to go against His own perfect nature! God is able to do all things, excepting to contradict Himself. But the moral law, though it must *bind* Him, does not limit Him, because it is He, — not an outside constraint upon Him, but a part of Him. But the arbitrary theory of forgiveness asserts that the moral law is only of force with men, — that we cannot reason from it to the dealings of God. (As if this did not also cut away the ground

from beneath our own moral conduct as well!) It asserts that God forgives some men solely because He arbitrarily *chooses*, not in any way because it is *in His nature* so to do. So it contrives *expedients* for winning the forgiveness which rests on only one condition in reality. It forges elaborately wrought keys of dogmatic creeds to open the kingdom of heaven with; but they are too intricate for the simple wards, which can be unlocked with the plain key of love and trust. It takes the dear name of Christ as a substitute instead of a succor in our saving, and really makes God solely a ruler whose sentence is to be escaped, instead of a loving Father.

3. The only theory of the Divine forgiveness which will hold in face of the New Testament, or of a true idea of the nature of God as drawn from that of man, or of the moral law, or of the needs of our own souls, is that which makes forgiveness a part of God's fatherhood. His all-embracing love is the only thing which will break the stony silence of nature's unforgiving laws, or solve the riddles in which human in-

genuity has involved the free grace of God. If I have never cared for my child it is probably a mystery to me to see a mother's tenderness with the fractious complainings of her infant. A restless, fretful creature, why does he not make her as miserable as himself? It is just that the mother-heart overflows in a tide large enough to drown her own discomfort, and to float the very resistance and rebellion of her child. Does God make the spirit of the woman larger than His own? Was not the love in Him before it was in her? "*As* one whom his mother comforteth, so will I comfort you, saith the Lord." Or what shall we make of the good tidings which is by Jesus Christ? His gospel is that God loves us, that He "loved us before we loved Him." And all his precepts are links in that golden chain which binds earth to heaven. And his life is the transparent medium through which the loving-kindness of God shines. If God's forgiving love be not true, we must change the definition of love altogether. His forgiveness is not shut up in the narrow limit of our own thought of Him, not bought for you or me and not for another. It is wider than the heavens and deeper than the sea, and takes in *all* His children. And man's offences cannot take him out of God's care and love.

But, it is said, this doctrine diminishes the evil of sin. Not so, excepting in so far as it diminishes the *quantity* of sin by saving men from its power. For the Divine forgiveness does not ignore or make light of *the fact* of sin. It rests first of all upon a condition on the human side, — the plain condition of sincere repentance. We cannot *receive* forgiveness until we wish to *take it*. And repentance is not an idle mood of the mind; it is a disposition going down to the very depths of the soul and "dividing the joints from the marrow," — as profound as the evil we have done. Till we have that, though God is forgiving, yet are we not forgiven, any more than a man with bandaged eyes can walk by daylight, though the sun pours its flood of day around him.

But, it is said, this is a dangerous condition on which to give so great a gift. Dangerous the principle may be for application to human governments, but precisely *because* they are *human*. They cannot test the genuineness of the repentance. But God can read the heart, and knows with unerring certainty the reality of the reformation. The forgiveness of men is at any rate one-sided and partial, colored with their own imperfections, affected by fancy and whim, by prejudice and interest. The forgiveness of God is the pure white ray of light from His own throne. And there is a forgiveness by men which does not even have any moral value whatsoever, — that " social condonation " which lets offences go simply because it cannot be at the trouble of remembering them. A keen critic of human nature has observed how unfair this is: " The best justice of the world is served out in very rude earthen vessels." For example, " Fraud in a merchant or a lawyer is a much more serious mischief than want of veracity in a soldier. But not so does society punish." It has an arbitrary standard of rewards and punishments of its own. Now there is no " condoning " in the heavenly forgiveness, because there is no imperfection in God. He does not forgive by *overlooking* the offences of His children, but by looking *through and through* them with a loving-kindness and tender mercy which can see the first dawn of repentance and can chasten even sinners "as sons." It is because there is no hiding of our inmost souls from God that we are sure that "He is faithful and just to forgive us our sins and to cleanse us from all unrighteousness."

And here comes in the reconciling work of Jesus Christ. The primary point of that work consists in disclosing the Divine love. To reveal God is to reconcile men. This is the atoning work of the Saviour, — bringing at one our human hearts and the Father by "showing us the Father." He who read the penitent spirit of the poor sinful woman who washed his feet with her tears, and whom the publicans and sinners rose up to call blessed, — *he* makes the tender pity of our God a visible fact, which cannot be blurred or winked away, and shows how perfect justice and perfect love can be reconciled. This is the side of Christ's work which it concerns us to know.

Forgiveness. — The Divine Side. 151

Besides, the Christian doctrine is that God is not an *impassible* God. He hears His children when they cry to Him; He pities them when they suffer; and though He wrap Himself in silence and darkness, He is still their *Father*. To forgive is in the essence of this infinite Being; it is a part of His full happiness. A Jewish parable in the Talmud relates that when God was about to create man, His different attributes pleaded with Him. "Create him not," said Truth, "for he will sin against Thy law of truth continually." "Create him not," said Justice; "for he will only deserve Thy condemnation." "Create him not," said Peace; "for he will bring discord and ruin everywhere." "Create him, O Father," said Mercy; "for he will give opportunity to show Thy mercy."

But it may be asked how this doctrine of the Divine forgiveness affects the fact of *punishment?* It does not affect *the fact*, it affects *the aspect* of it. The penalty of sin is still needful, but it is not a *vindictive* penalty. It is wrapped up in every sin as surely as the harvest sleeps in the seed. But it is chastening and remedial. As the child must feel the scorch of flame to learn to dread it, so the soul learns from the *hurt* of sin to fear *sin itself*. But when I learn from the Gospel that God is still my forgiving Father, the *sting* of my suffering is gone. Though the soul should go scarred by it through all eternity, it may in its very crippled state lean more closely upon God. And thus the truth of future punishment and the truth of future salvation are reconciled. "He shall save His people," says the Scripture, not from the *consequences of their sins*, but "from *their sins*." His forgiveness will lift us out of the settled despair of evil habits, above the enslaving bondage of some passion or weakness which has enthralled the whole nature; and though we remember it and go on bruised and faint from its thraldom, we are transplanted into new conditions. Now there is hope and life.

A favorite school of thought in our own day meets this position by denying the fundamental truth which lies at its basis. It is claimed by some that there is really no alienation between man and God. The idea of sin is a dyspeptic phantom, and is to be banished by following out the impulses of our human nature. Well, that experiment was pretty thoroughly tried in the dark and sinful centuries before the Christian helps were known to men. The fact about human nature is simply that while, on the one hand, it is not "totally depraved," on the other it is not totally divine. It is a very mixed thing, and because mixed it needs the harmonizing power of the spirit of God. Chaos contained a great many good elements, but they needed the breath of that Spirit moving "upon the waters."

But, it is said, we will bear the punishment of our sins, if we have any, without flinching. It would be the part of a coward to do the wrong and refuse to pay its price. Yes! bear it, — no fear but there will be *enough* to bear. But the question is not *whether* you shall bear it, but *how* you shall bear it. You may have sinned, but you are still *a child of God*. Do not you wish to be reconciled, to feel that even your wrong does not stand between you and your Father's love?

The sense of our need of *that* is deeper in the human heart than any philosophical theory. That church which has taken the wants of the soul and made even a false answer to them its tower of strength, has recognized this in its doctrine of *absolution*. The Protestant enters the vast pile of St. Peter's with admiration and wonder, yet does not feel in all its splendor the solemn presence which he seeks till he stands beneath the soaring dome and looks round on the circle of confessionals inscribed each with the name of a different language, inviting wanderers from many lands to lay their burdens down. Then he feels that it is a faint and material type of the refuge which God offers everywhere and always to His children. For everywhere under the blue dome of the infinite heavens the door of confession is open to His children. No human ear need come between to hear the prayer, no human voice to utter the pardon. It only needs a seeking heart.

The doctrine of God's forgiveness lies at the root of the religious life.

1. It gives a ground for *hope*, because it gives

Forgiveness. — The Divine Side. 155

an opportunity to start anew, feeling that the future is not mortgaged beyond remedy to our error-laden past.

2. It gives a ground for *faith*, because it reveals to us a God whom we can trust and love. It makes *repentance* a stepping-stone to truer living, and *prayer* a real cry to one who really answers.

3. It takes hold on life itself, to make it divine by breathing into it the same spirit of forgiving love. Men have learned this hardest of all the graces by trying to imitate God. This is the spirit which glowed in the Christian martyrs. John Huber, a distinguished Huguenot galley-slave, has recorded the following experience: —

"We arrived one night at a little town, chained, my wife and my children with fourteen galley slaves. The priests came to us, offering freedom on condition that we abjured. We agreed to preserve a profound silence. After them came the women and children of the place, who covered us with mud. I made my little party fall on their knees, and we put up this prayer in which all the fugitives joined: 'Gracious God, who seest the wrongs to which we are hourly exposed, give us strength to support them, and to forgive in charity those who wrong us. Strengthen us from good even unto better.'"[1]

"From good even unto better." This is the aspiration of the human soul. And from better unto *best* we still look up adoring at the perfect fulness of forgiving love which is in the bosom of our Heavenly Father. When the Pharisees heard Jesus, they said, "Who is this, that *forgiveth sins* also?" But all men since have recognized in this very thing the sure evidence that he is the Son of God. And so far as we are touched with his spirit, we shall rise into his likeness, and "forgive, as we also are forgiven."

[1] Smiles's Huguenots.

FORGIVENESS.—THE HUMAN SIDE.

VIII.

II. FORGIVENESS. — THE HUMAN SIDE.

Forgive us our debts, as we forgive our debtors. —
MATT. vi. 12.

Then came Peter to him and said, Lord, how oft shall my brother sin against me, and I forgive him? till seven times? Jesus saith unto him, I say not unto thee, until seven times: but, until seventy times seven.
MATT. xviii. 21, 22.

THE apostle who was to be entrusted with the keeping of the keys of the kingdom of heaven probably thought that he had gone to the outermost verge of the requirement of Christ, when he spoke of *seven* times as the limit required. And certainly that was *more than* seven times as many as the natural impulse of the human heart requires. But Peter was like one who having launched upon a bay, land-locked and limited, finds himself borne on by the sweep of a vast tide that feels the pulse of the ocean, rising and falling on the waves of mightier waters, contained only by the blue infinitude above and the blue infinitude below, and by the edge of the round world. So far does the doctrine of forgiveness, as taught by Christ, open out beyond any narrow idea of it. I believe it to be a just statement, that this doctrine of forgiveness is a distinctively *Christian* truth, — one of the characteristic features of the Gospel. The Hebrews had glimmers and gleams of it; within limits and under definitions, it was not unknown to the purest ethical and religious systems of antiquity; but forgiveness *with the Christian reach* and *for the Christian reasons* belongs in the Christian religion alone. Simply because it seems unattainable, except to those who have the light of Jesus Christ to see it by, and the help of Jesus Christ to reach it by. On the plane of our average life, to forgive an enemy or an injury seems out of our sphere. But if there be any practical duty enforced by Christ and his apostles, it is this strange, plain, hard duty, to *forgive*. Over and over again, as if they feared lest it should be forgotten, they return to it, in epistle and gospel, bidding us "forgive one another, even as God for Christ's sake hath forgiven us," or telling us earnest parables, like that of "the unmerciful servant," or making us in the Lord's Prayer ask God Himself that His forgiveness of us may be as our forgiveness of "them that trespass against us." And here it is noteworthy that this part of the Lord's Prayer is the only part which Christ thinks it needful to explain, as Saint Augustine points out. Probably because he recognizes that it is so hard for us, and that we need every strength that can be given us, he says, "*For if ye forgive not men their trespasses, neither will your heavenly Father forgive you your trespasses.*" The only way to make a hard duty easy is to bring God into it; and the harder it is, the closer must the thought of Him be interwoven with it.

And I say again the spirit of forgiveness is hard to attain. For consider how great and utter a virtue of soul it is. In its true meaning *forgiving* is *the giving away* of an offence; and the Greek has the same idea even more delicately expressed; it is the *sending away* of a thing, that is, the making it to disappear from between two persons. Some offence has risen between man and man; it stands like an ugly incarnation of evil in the way of their seeing each other; they cannot look round it or through it; they cannot speak naturally to each other across its black shadow. Now it is not a light matter, to be brought about with a word, or in some momentary amiable mood when the world goes particularly well with us, to exorcise this enemy of our peace, to send it utterly away from between us two, so that the sunshine can fall broad and free between us again, and kindly human fellowship can grasp hands across the closed-up gulf. Yet *that*, and no less than *that*, is perfect forgiveness. Oh, it is hard to do it; harder than to pray, for the soul cannot help melting sometimes at the thought of God's goodness, and then it speaks to Him as its Father; harder than to do justly, for there is an instinctive desire in men to "do what is *about right*," as the phrase is, and this is not far from doing what is *quite* right. But to *forgive*, to silence the tingling blood which mounts at insult or injustice, and still to keep the spirit of human love and of Divine pity closer to our hearts than our offence, this requires the heroism of self-conquest. For a wrong is a most obstinate thing; it will not "down" at our bidding. "Only by prayer and fasting goeth out this kind of devil," by the prayerful temper of a holy mind, by the fasting of a perfect subduing of self.

Now this difficulty is not felt by untamed human nature. On the contrary, the savage has no ethical idea more deeply engraven on his barbarous code of morals than the notion that revenge is good in and for itself. No duty is more sacred to him than that of repaying his enemy to the uttermost. The wild man of the prairie counts his foe's life no too great price for a stolen beast. Nay, the frontiersman, who perhaps was sprinkled with Christian baptism in some quiet New England village, takes kindly to the ways of the savage and forgets that there is "a more excellent way." What is much of the so-called "code of honor" but the relics of the barbarian that lurks under the painted garb of civilization? Even nations which call themselves Christian can often find no better method of giving or taking reparation for one injury than by inflicting another, and must write their treaties of peace in bloody letters, to be read by the flames of burning cities, and uttered from the throats of volleying cannon. Religion, in its primary stage, so far from banishing this notion of revenge, intensified it, and had altars to Hate and prayers for Vengeance. And it was reserved for Jesus Christ to proclaim the repeal of the law which Moses had given in the highest and purest religion of antiquity, not because it was perfect, but "because of the hardness of the Jews' hearts,"—"an eye for an eye and a tooth for a tooth."

In all this there was at least a very intense earnestness. It was a fixed and clear moral law of society which defined forgiveness by leaving no place for it in the recognized system of life and duty. Modern civilized manners have refined many things (though how far they have *changed* their essential nature, is another question); and so here. They have made it one of the proprieties of life to forgive our enemies and our injuries *in general*, although when it comes to *particular* instances the case is very different. In these days a malignant hostility, even for a cause, is regarded, if made too public, as a breach of the social decencies, and men sometimes consider this a great proof of the world's advance toward perfection. But I apprehend that the only thing which it *surely* proves is, that the temper of civilized man is less fiery than in a simpler state. The volcano loses its molten glow whose fierceness will liquefy the very rocks; but it hardens into solid lava and is covered by an ashy crust. And so the habits of men may have grown cooler, but less impressible to good as well as evil, and covered with the ashes of an indifference which is nigh akin to deadness of the mind.

Whatever may be said of the progress of the human race, I apprehend that no one can deny that civilization, considered as a power in humanity apart from religion, tends rather to increase the spirit of selfish indifference in the individual than to excite any glow of self-sacrifice. And so there is a forgiveness which is no *true* forgiveness, but is simply an easy temper, letting things go because it is the least troublesome way. It is only a shallow cure for a very deep-seated evil of spirit, thus to suppose that a state of mind can take care of itself; and it is to be feared that we often please ourselves with ourselves very mistakenly, giving ourselves much credit for what is really mere laziness of feeling, forgiving that we may not be at the pains of keeping a grudge (and it is the most expensive thing that we *can* keep). Said the keen La Rochefoucauld: "Reconciliation with our enemies is only a desire to render our condition better, a weariness of war and a fear of some evil event." Or we use that idle proverb about "forgiving and forgetting," as if by not thinking about a grievance it would wear itself away with time. But *time* cannot regenerate the soul, and it is there that the spirit of forgiveness must be found, the spirit which will not merely *forget*, that is, let a thing slip away into the background of our memory, only to start forth again when it can annoy us most, but will *forgive*, that is, send away and banish utterly that which frets us.

But these delusive counterfeits of the Christian virtue of forgiveness, though wanting in any moral value, are harmless in comparison with the hypocrisy which sets out at the same time to reap the religious benefit of forgiving the sin against us and to preserve its unrelenting gripe upon the sinner. One of those hard, grasping natures who are sometimes born into the world lay a-dying, after an unlovely life. The little religion which he had, had come to him not as the sunlight comes to a fair prospect, to kindle upon it a yet fairer beauty, but as it shines on a barren stone, to bring out all its wrinkled stoniness. So the hypocritical religion which he professed had seemed only to give a new excuse for all the perverseness which was in him. He was dying, and he knew it, and sent for his minister, to make sure of his passport yonder.

But the clergyman was a faithful man, and knew the weak places in his spiritual patient's character, and told him that he must forgive his enemies as he himself hoped to be forgiven. He called to him his son: "Well, *I* must forgive such an one; but my curse be upon you if *you* do." There is something near to blasphemy in it yet we may well press home to ourselves the question if it is not after all too much after our own inclination to forgive with the lips or outwardly, while we cherish and nurse an undying grudge in the heart; yes, and feel in our hearts a sort of pride in so doing as a manly and spirited act.

The true forgiveness must be a part of the very temper of the soul itself; not merely a word or act, but a disposition. It is a Christian virtue, because it belongs to the Christianized soul. There are virtues which belong on the *natural* plane, for example, courage, fidelity, truth; there are others which belong on the *supernatural* plane, that is, which are a part of the soul that has come into conscious relations to God, and is lifted by the Divine strength above its unassisted powers. Then man rises out of the limitations which have constrained him on the heavenward side, and *hopes*, as one whose horizon is bounded only by the sky, and *loves*, as seeing the immortal in the mortal, and *forgives*, because he is capable of self-sacrifice and self-forgetfulness.

But do I then seem to be urging an unattainable or mysterious virtue? Perhaps some of the difficulties which beset the practical application of this virtue will diminish if we pause here to ask exactly *what it is* which we are called on at one time or another in life to forgive. That which in a general principle of conduct appears too high for our reach, is often made more easy in its special applications.

The grievances which annoy us may be classified under three heads: —

1. There are the offences against our *convenience*. In a world so complicated as this in which we live, and where we jostle so closely against one another, it would be strange if all went exactly to suit us, since we were not consulted in the putting of society together, and

we are not the only persons concerned in it. Notwithstanding, a large part of the troubles of mankind arise from a failure to make allowance for this self-evident fact.

But the want of tolerance goes much beyond this, and touches inconveniences which are merely of the whim or fancy. You do not like the tone of a man's voice, the shape of his figure, the manner in which he manages his own affairs. And why *should* you? All these are *his*, not *yours*. Notwithstanding, many of the best people in the world take their friends' peculiarities so much to heart that they can hardly keep on good terms with them, and find it hard to forgive Providence for making them so at all. Nor is this a light matter for laughter only; it really hinders much of the free joy of life, and raises a multitude of petty hurts to a serious dignity, as a swarm of summer insects, which singly are brushed aside disregarding, in the mass sting and goad to distraction.

2. But the troubles are much deeper which arise from offences *against our rights*. For these aggrieve not only our comfort, but our

pride. Still it is not, necessarily, that a wrong has been done us knowingly; it is only that we had a larger claim than is allowed. Hence grow most of the quarrels that embitter life.

It is almost safe to say that no fault can be only on *one* side; and if we would try in any matter *first* to find where the blame lies at *our* door, we should often stop on the threshold of *that*, and never get beyond it. Besides, who shall measure the amount of offences against our rights which simply arise from *false expectations*, from demanding of the world more consideration, or more pay, than fairly belongs to us, or than we are willing to bestow? But set the case at its worst, that one has been injured in what is justly his; still, to nurse the injury is only putting it out to interest. It were better to forgive, if any one could do it for so mean a reason, and to wipe out the annoyance with the remembrance. But the more common way is to defend doubtful rights of one's own by trespassing on the undoubted rights of others, and to get reparation after the manner of two kings who go to war about a barren corner of territory, at a cost of men enough to people it and treasure enough to buy it ten times over.

3. Yet another kind of annoyance, which is yet near akin to this, is from offences against *God's requirements through us;* that is, we constitute ourselves representatives of the Divine authority, and try to find an act of rebellion against *that* in every breach of our privilege. Like the Oriental monarchs whose names are so sacred that they cannot be spoken on pain of death, we wrap the cloak of sacredness round our personality, and identify our own welfare with the eternal laws, which may not be transgressed. To trespass against *us* is to commit treason against Heaven. And so there are some men who wage a kind of religious war against mankind, serenely confident that they are vindicating the Divine justice in their own wrongs. It must be said, too, that sometimes the very interest in a great moral question will lead to an identification of one's self with the neglected truth or cause, which produces an amazing bitterness of personal feeling.

To separate the sure from the uncertain truth, to weigh other men's motives fairly, to allow for differences of judgment, requires a breadth and calmness of vision not easy to attain. And there is no intensity of unforgivingness so utter as when one would blast not a sin alone, but *the sinner* with the fires of Heaven's wrath. "When John Huss was at the stake to be burnt, his eye fixed upon a poor, plain country fellow, whom he observed to be busier than the rest, and to run oftener to fetch more and more fagots to burn him; and he said thereupon no more but this, *O sancta simplicitas.*" Burnings and hangings, inquisitions and crusades, religious scandals and ecclesiastical schisms, have all grown out of this feeling of personal responsibility for the Divine justice. Have you never heard it said, "I cannot forgive such or such a moral attitude toward some great principle"? But are you *asked* to forgive it, or to make it your own matter at all? Surely, if you make sure that your own heart is thoroughly in sympathy with God's truth, you can trust God Himself to take care of the rest.

Now it is not difficult to admit that of all these kinds of injury it should really be no hard thing to forgive, (*a*) offences against our *convenience*, because we have *no pre-eminent right* in the matter; (*b*) offences against our rights, *because* we have a right in the matter, and can therefore afford to be magnanimous; (*c*) offences against God, because we need all our strength to keep ourselves in God's ways and must not spend it in wrath against those who have wandered from them. But we have not yet touched the really difficult point in the question of forgiveness. It is put in a word. Can we forgive an act of *moral turpitude?* Is it possible to wipe out the memory of a wrong which has been done us, in which there was meanness, or double-dealing, or dishonor? I answer, *No.* The Christian gospel does not confuse the lines between right and wrong; it renders them sharp and clear; it does not enjoin a weak, easy good-nature, which can be imposed upon indefinitely, but moral insight. If your friend has really betrayed his trust, or has been fair-spoken to your face and a foe to your back, you know that there is falsehood in him; you cannot any more treat him as a true man, if you are yourself true. But you must make sure, and *trebly* sure, that you do not do him wrong. Remember that it is the hardest matter to judge *motives*. Suppose, for example, that one has spoken cruelly of you. It may be for the good of a cause in whose way you seem to him to be standing; it may be a fair condemnation of your own doubtful conduct. "Faithful are the wounds of a friend," says the Scripture; and criticism, even when it seems harsh and unfair, will often have a wholesome lesson for us. But if it be indeed the worst that can happen, and you are betrayed, and the seeming friendship is a lie, — what then? Manifestly, the friendship is dead; bury it out of your sight; yet bury it tenderly, for the sake of the love and honor which you once believed were in it. But you can still *forgive,* so far as your own heart is concerned, and send the wrong away from *you.* *The wrong* you can banish from between you. *The penalty* of the wrong must remain, — your friend has lost you. Yet even there may there be a resurrection of that which seemed buried forever, if the sin is washed out by the tears of repentance. As has been said, "The offender must *send* the wrong away, as well as the offended." Yet we need not wait for *that;* we can banish the bitterness and lose the sense of personal wrong in grief for the fault of an erring soul.

"A person told F. Ravignan that he had been calumniated by a false friend. 'It is certainly a great affliction,' answered the father, with an expression of the tenderest compassion; 'but is there not something *better* within you, to forget and to pardon? Raise yourself by prayer to this higher level of faith, and then be happy and go in peace.' The counsel was adopted and peace restored."[1]

This is the Christian spirit, which does not *count* grievances, but *rises above* them, and tries to see life as God sees it, and can "suffer, yet be strong."

We should find it easier, as well as nobler, to cultivate the spirit of forgiveness of real

[1] Life of F. Ravignan, p. 392.

wrongs, when such there be that we suffer, if we tried to put ourselves more in the place of the other person. For then you would find that whatever you suffer is really far outweighed by the loss which he suffers. He may not know it, or may be only dimly conscious of the murky atmosphere in his own heart; but, none the less, no man can do another a wilful wrong without infinite hurt in his own soul. You would pity your worst enemy and try to help him, if you saw him in bodily peril. Will you not pity if you see him on fire with anger, or seeking to cheat you and perhaps succeeding, and if he succeeds doomed to carry with him, until he repents, the burden of a mean and fraudulent act, and a conscience which will plague him if awake, and if asleep is ten times more to be pitied.

Yield to this pity when it stirs within your heart, and you are safe. For then the very dew from heaven descends on your own soul, and instead of being a dry and thirsty land, where no water is, it will be full of living springs. It is God Himself stirring in your spirit, helping your prayer for the forgiveness which you know you need from Him, every day you live, for sins of omission and of commission,—answering that prayer by the very fact that you are put in a mood to pray it.

"If thou bring thy gift to the altar, and there rememberest that thy brother hath aught against thee, leave there thy gift before the altar; first be reconciled to thy brother, and then come and offer thy gift," said our Master.

And how much more potent are the inducements which are on us thus to forgive than the force of any wrong can be!

For we ourselves have *lived*, and having tasted life we know how hard it is *not* to sin against one's neighbor. Experience should teach us tolerance. In these paths where it is so easy to stumble, so difficult to walk with sure and steady step, we should rather learn to reach out a helping hand to a brother than to push him further if he fall. Says Marcus Aurelius: "It is right that man should love those who have offended him. He will do so when he remembers that all men are his relations, and that it is through ignorance and involuntarily that they sin,—and then we all die so soon." He died sixteen centuries ago, but the golden thought lives to teach us charity. The sense of human frailty should prevent us from crowding this little span of life with hates and discords that leave no room for serener thoughts.

And shall we wait for that time of silence to forgive when we can do no otherwise? Not alone the sense of *mortality*, but the trust in *immortality* would bid us rise now to the height of a forgiving spirit. For we are compounded not alone of dust, but of a divine spirit, and this earthly life is a part of the heavenly. We should therefore see in things which vex us their divine element, — "a soul of goodness in things evil." We should learn to trust cheerfully in human nature, in that nature which God has given to us all as a power for strength and good. Old Michael Feneberg, in his school, "reconciled two boys who would not speak to each other by setting them down to their porridge with only one spoon between them." Somewhat so are we all set down to a common work and calling here together, too close in brotherhood and fellowship to permit any grudge to come between us.

Nay, not alone on the side of human fellowship, but on the side of God's loving-kindness, does the principle of forgiveness come to us. For the strong sense of God's love for us should melt our hearts into a fervor of love which can see His children in all men, and feel His pardon moving *us* to pardon.

Forgiveness is the *duty of sinners*. In the presence of the perfect justice which we have offended, and the absolute purity before which the very angels bow themselves to the dust and cry, "Unclean, unclean," knowing that we too deserve to suffer, humility should teach us a long-suffering charity. "He that cannot forgive others," says Lord Herbert, "breaks the bridge over which he must pass himself; for every man has need to be forgiven."

Forgiveness is the *obedience of disciples*. For it is in the law of Jesus Christ that we should forgive our enemies, and pray for those who despitefully use us, and return good for evil.

Forgiveness is the *privilege of God's children*.

It is a gift whose exercise is the sign and pledge of our divinity, of the victory of His loving spirit in our hearts. Said Martin Boos: "People think it a weakness to forgive an insult. Then God would be the weakest in heaven and on earth; for no one in heaven or earth forgives so much as He." Where His children are made in His spiritual likeness, they can "forgive seven times or seventy times seven;" for it is not a question of *arithmetic*, but a question of *grace*. A duty, an obedience, a privilege, we can forgive from fear, from law, or from love. And "love is the fulfilling of the law," and "perfect love casteth out fear."

We can see why it is that the world is so strangely full of occasions for forgiveness, and the frequent need of this virtue is ever upon us. It is because God seeks to educate us in those qualities which are like Himself. Out of the very vexations and perplexities of life best spring the self-denial, the love, whose home is in the bosom of God. Not sufficient is that answer which a deaf and dumb person wrote with his pencil to the question, "What is your idea of forgiveness?" "It is the odor which flowers yield when trampled on." It is more than passive submission; it is actively rising superior, and the fragrance which it yields is not the perfume of a crushed nature, but the bloom and beauty of a strong and victorious soul.

But as we speak of forgiveness, out of the far past across the Christian ages looks forth upon us One not dimly seen though so far away. His life is a precept even stronger than his word. And while we listen we feel that we can obey, — there is that in him which draws us so earnestly after him. The atoning love which shines forth in him brings at one men with men, and men with God. The reconciled soul forgets its hatreds and its discords in Christ Jesus. And the words which breathe from his cross tenderly touch our hearts with a sense of our own need of pardon, and with loving-kindness for those whose worst offences against us are as nothing beside the world's sins against the Sinless One. "Father, forgive them; they know not what they do."

LEAD US NOT INTO TEMPTATION.

IX.

LEAD US NOT INTO TEMPTATION.

And lead us not into temptation. — MATT. vi. 13.

THE grave problem of the relation of evil to our moral consciousness has forced itself on the consideration of ethical thinkers ever since men began to think at all. Why do we feel that it is wrong to yield to temptation? Why *do* we yield to it, feeling it to be wrong? What is the use of it?

The true value and discipline of temptation is sometimes obscured by a theory often held by thinkers, the theory of pure optimism, which makes even the worst only the fermentation of the best. It is so sure that God is over all, and that where He is all will be well, that it falls into the mistake of supposing that every step of the process is also good. "Hell itself is but heaven in the making." But this view labors under the fatal weakness that it blurs moral distinctions. If it makes no difference after all, in the long run, whether one has been sinner or saint, if when we stumble we fall *upward* as far as those climb who never fall at all, why should it be deemed such a grave matter if we stumble? Sin becomes not even a case of *arrested* development, but only of *individual* development, — that is, in the logical results of this speculative view. Besides, this view impugns the character of God, by making Him to have created a moral nature in us which is repelled by the moral evils which, according to this theory, He not merely *permits*, but which are a part of His moral order of the world. The moral nature of man and the system of the moral universe do not ring true to each other, as they should, since both come from the hand of God.

But another partial and distorted conception of the nature and function of evil is contained in the *necessitarian* theory. I do not so much mean the stern old system of rigid Calvinism, which attributed all to the arbitrary will of the Creator, and believed that he created some men to be lost, and others to be saved, according to His own hidden purpose. The grim old theologians who worked out this explanation of the mysteries of evil, failed to see how completely it abolishes all responsibility for sin, while it leaves all its punishment,— because it does away with moral freedom. The doctrine of necessity to-day, however, follows a different course, and rests not on the metaphysics of God, but on material phenomena. It does away with sin by doing away with responsibility, in making all moral facts the outcome of physical conditions. Man is but a curiously wrought and animated machine, and grinds out virtue or vice according to his conditions, as unblamably as a cotton-loom weaves sound or sleazy fabrics according to the material furnished it. As M. Taine states it: " Les actions extrêmes de l'homme proviennent, non de sa volonté, mais de son nature." Now, no thoughtful person can deny the limits of moral freedom; but that is a very different thing from denying the freedom *within* those limits. Granted that this is a question of facts, not of mere sentiment. But sound sentiment is *also a fact*, and has a right to be considered, until disproved by other facts. So long as material science says "Not proven" to the assumption that moral and spiritual phenomena are but links in the materialistic chain, so long the freedom of the will has a right to assert itself, and the consciousness which is a "law of the mind," will deny that it is subject to the "law of the members." It would be a kind of fatalism very quieting to the moral sense, to believe that we are simply to work out our own nature, good and bad equally, as may happen, or, rather, that which we *call* good and that which we *call* bad. But the machine turns out scruples, regrets, twinges of conscience, as well as passions and desires; and we cannot take one part and leave the other part.

The Christian doctrine of temptation goes beneath both of these superficial theories of Evil. It does not undertake to decide the speculative question of the weight of determining causes, such as physical conditions, inheritance, and the like; it *does* say that freedom of choice is also a determining cause, and can mould and shape life holily, justly, purely, *within* these other conditions, if not *above* them. It asserts, as strongly as the most resolute optimist, that God rules, and all must be well. But it says that, because He is able to bring good out of evil, it does not follow that evil is a part of His Providence. As Mr. Chaney has said: "Evil may be *good for something*, but it is not therefore *good*," — good to discipline the soul, to show forth God's power, — good to fight against and conquer; but not therefore good to yield to and obey.

The true function of temptation in our human life was stated by Jesus in one striking pictorial sentence, in a conversation with his disciples, when he warned Peter that temptation was the very *sifting* of the soul. "Simon, Satan hath desired to have you, that he might sift you as wheat."

How vivid the picture which it must have called up to his disciples' minds, that primitive process which they had seen every harvest time since they could remember! There is a familiar picture, representing that Oriental custom. A woman tall and free, with garments girded close and arms raised high above her head, stands where the winds blow, holding aloft a sieve from which the golden grain falls in a heap at her feet, clean and pure, while the chaff is blown abroad, and only worthless, unclean lumps of clay or stones remain in the sieve.

It is a living parable of that which Christ seeks to teach by the illustration. So, he would tell us, temptation is no light thing; it shakes the soul with a perpetual disquiet and annoy; it will not let it remain in peace, any more than the grain which the energetic holder shakes in air can sleep in its receptacle. The winds of heaven, cold and searching, must blow through it.

Every test must be applied which will sift the golden grain of character, sweet and wholesome, and free it from the chaff of a light-minded and frivolous spirit, which the breezes may blow where they will,—from the lumpish and earthy sins which only by this thorough winnowing can be purged away from the wheat of the soul. And if the sifting reveals the substance of the character to be but poor stuff after all, at least the test has been applied; the opportunity has been given. We are revealed honestly, as we are, as we have chosen to be. And how searching the tests are by which the whole being of man and woman is tried and proved in this world of God!

I see a man standing in his place in the business community. It is a place of trust, directly or indirectly; for if one is not the agent of another employer in so many words, certainly every man is under bonds to society to do the work which he undertakes to do in society fairly and honestly, whether it be to make goods or to sell them, to keep accounts, or practise law, or heal men's bodies, or preach the gospel. And the tempter comes to him with the subtle suggestion that he commit a breach of trust for selfish ends. It will never be found out; it can all be made right next day or next week; if it should ever come to light, it will only be what other men are doing all the time. Success will justify it. It is only to lie to the customer by saying a little more or a little less than the truth; it is only to mingle a little quackery in your law or medicine or ministry, just in order, you know, to induce mankind to take the wholesome work which you can do for them when they once believe in you; it is only to use other people's money, without their knowledge or consent, for your own purposes, while it would otherwise be lying idle. Perhaps he hearkens to the subtle tempter; and then, to his horror, he finds that one sin opens the door to another and another. He cannot turn back if he would. If he gains that which he seeks, he loses that which he never dreamed of losing, human respect and his own sense of character; often and often, he loses that which he staked his soul on, too. Perhaps he stands fast by his sense of right, and bides the sifting as he may. It is not easy to resist temptation which hardly seems evil, nor to see other men passing him in the race. But the strong wind blows away light purposes and trivial desires from his soul; the shakings of his temptations winnow out the solid weight of character; and he remains strong and proved by his trial.

A young man feels the stress and strain of the passions which are a part of his nature, given him to be moulded into a power for God and for good. It is so easy to yield but for a little, to look a little way into the darker side of the world, to know something of "*life.*" But it is like the gentle tug with which the waters of Niagara above the rapids entice a boat away from its moorings, to float on the pleasant and prosperous stream. Floating with the current is so easy that it cannot be hard by and by to row against it. But what is that dull roar in the distance? It is the cataract of ruin; and if perchance it is not yet too late, it will only be by the effort of his whole manhood that he comes safe to land, and then at a place far lower down than that where he yielded first.

Thank God for him who holds fast by his Christian principle, and shuns the very beginnings of evil, and endures the blessed ignorance of evil which he will later account one of his best rewards, and suffers the mocking laugh of the disappointed fiend. For so he lays the sure foundations of a manhood which is honorable because it can honor itself. No ugly blot hidden in its own heart mars its peace. No sudden temptation can sweep it away from its virtue, because it anchored long ago on the rock of duty and conscience.

The call of charity comes to man or woman, in another way, — a temptation to good. But it is possible here, too, to misunderstand the voice that speaks. One can pretend to one's self that it spoke to his neighbor and not to him, that it said "to-morrow, and not to-day," that it was a mistake to take it for God's voice, since it was only a human one. One can let the luxury of pity be a substitute for the earnestness of deed. Or one can be "obedient to the heavenly vision," and taste the sweetness of divinest charity, and give service, even if money be wanting, and, with or without the money, the sympathy which is also a form of charitable service.

Lead Us not into Temptation. 195

The test of *opportunity* is a very searching one. It finds out the weak places and foibles in the character; but it also finds and perfects the solid worth which is as pure gold.

Another person has temptations of a more inward sort, but not less real on that account. Doubts and questionings, some of which can never be fully solved in this world, paralyze the soul's action. This is the great temptation of many a thoughtful person. He sees much that seems contrary to reason and justice; he finds difficulties in the way of faith; and he falls to desponding and despairing, instead of doing the work of life.

And it must not be forgotten that the spiritual temptations, the *tryings* which beset us on the side of religion, are of a most searching kind. Religious indolence solicits the easy, and religious pride the self-satisfied, and religious criticism the censorious spirit. No soul can be so lofty as to rise above all these risks; for none in becoming devout or holy cease thereby to be men. The greatest of the apostles, he whom we may call the greatest man that ever lived, has told us that he had a "thorn in the flesh," and thrice he besought the Lord that it might depart from him; but the only answer was, "My grace is sufficient for thee."

One is tempted, we may almost say, once for all, and has but a single mortal combat with his foe, and never again is in the same peril. There are moments when a gallantry of conscience, so to speak, seems to raise one permanently to a higher level of moral purpose, and the soul always afterward stands in the attitude of pre-assured victory toward its special enemy.

Another is tempted, and has to fight the same battle over and over, a hundred times. Never winning a decisive victory, he is worried and worn by endless skirmishes. Some taint of passion, or some moral cowardice returns upon him, after months or years; and he is humiliated to find himself weaker than he had believed.

Now there are real dangers in all this.

1. The peril of *despondency* is one, — and it is

a very real temptation. It is very hard to become reconciled to the fact that circumstances seem made on purpose to thwart us. Are not these difficulties which so beset us in doing our simple duty proof of an ill-ordered world? They are in the constitution of the world, in the very *make* of our own souls. Can an overruling Providence have made everything to work so contrary to His perfect will?

Christianity meets this state of mind in the only way in which it can be met, by teaching that the Divine plan for human life has regard supremely to the growth of human character, while mere outward results count for very little. Easy successes, great works done with everything to favor us would be worth no more than they really cost us, — to be "carried to the skies on flowery beds of ease." The discipline of temptation is what we must have to toughen the moral fibre. How can the soul learn to choose good rather than evil, unless it has the evil presented to it as well as the good? This world mysterious? It is so; but far more incomprehensible would it be, if there were no temptation in it. For then would it lack one of the chief signs of the Providence which has made it the training-place of man. There is no room for despondency here. Nothing will do more than this very faintness of heart to thwart the accomplishment of His great will, which surely never meant that this world's perplexities should cause us to lose our heart, our hope, our faith.

2. Another danger, quite the opposite of this, yet quite as perilous, is the *worldly view* of this whole question. We may let ourselves think that since God has so ordered the circumstances of life, it can make no great difference how we take them. If He subjects you to temptation, can there be great harm, you say, in yielding to temptation? While we are in the world, we are a part of the world, and must take things as they are. Yes! but we must not be *taken by them*. This worldly philosophy of life might do well enough for us, if there were not *that* in us, which is greater than the world. For there still remains the

obstinate fact that you have an immortal soul; and the fact, greater still, that God Himself lives. To obey the weaker part of us, rather than the stronger, can never satisfy us; nor can *sin*, the consenting to a temptation which we might resist, ever be anything but displeasing to Him who is perfect Holiness and Goodness. When we are "overthrown in that wilderness" of fleshly appetite, or narrow selfishness, or passions that corrode the soul, we need not think to escape under His fancied indifference. We know our own true calling and His Nature far too well to do that.

3. Yet once more, we are often tempted *to impatience* under the ceaseless pressure of the temptations which seem to enter into life at every turn. Has God, we almost ask, *any right* to deal thus with His poor earthly children? He created us; He knows our weakness, our strange mingling of conscience and of desires that seem too strong for it. How can we reconcile all this with the thought of His justice and His mercy?

There is only one answer possible. He will

not lay upon us burdens greater than we are able to bear. We are not under the harrow of an irresistible Fate, but under the leading of a Loving Purpose. The *possibility* of giving way, indeed, there must be; else were the free-will, which we know if we know anything at all, only a delusion. It is better to have the chance of falling, that we may rise, than to be the puppet of destiny, even though beneficent. But the *power* of resisting is as great as the possibility of yielding; and if we yield it is in spite of the great plan of God.

Does temptation mortify you by teaching you your weakness? But the very smart of your conscience pleading with you not to yield, teaches that there is a God who cares that you should not. The trial has not taught all that it has to teach you, until you have learned also that He is able to *help* to the uttermost in time of need. "God writes straight," says the proverb, "on crooked lines."

All this applies to the *tryings* which God sends to us or permits for us; but we must not forget how large a part we have in the shaping of our own lives and that of those dearer to us than our own. God means that part of the answer to it should be given by ourselves, in resolutions and purposes, girded to resist the temptations which will be much or little to us as we may choose to have them.

If I may quote again the wholesome bitter of Mr. Ruskin ("Letters to the Clergy") : —

"No man can ask honestly or hopefully to be delivered from temptation, unless he has himself honestly and firmly determined to do the best he can to keep out of it. But in modern days, the first aim of all Christian parents is to place their children in circumstances where the temptations (which they are apt to call 'opportunities') may be as great and as many as possible, where the sight and promise of 'all these things' in Satan's gift may be brilliantly near, and where the act of 'falling down to worship me' may be partly concealed by the shelter, and partly excused as involuntary by the pressure, of the concurrent crowd."

But after all this is said, this prayer comes home to our need as does no other. "Lead us not into temptation," we say; and we must say it, if we know ourselves aright, as long as we live in this human world. Dante, in that great passage of his "Paradiso" where he describes the blessed ones in heaven praying our Lord's Prayer together, makes them stop when they come to this clause. They do not need it any longer. And we thank God for them that in His larger light they do not need to pray it. But *we* need it; and it is surely well that we cannot truly pray it for ourselves alone. The same brotherhood which was in the Prayer at its beginning is in it at the close. "Lead *us* not." It unites all in one danger, and makes the help of each needful before the All-seeing One for every other.

All this is beautifully said by Mr. Maurice in a passage which I cannot forbear to read:—

"Oh, strange and mysterious privilege, that some bed-ridden woman in a lonely garret, who feels that she is tempted to distrust the love and mercy of Him who sent His Son to die for the helpless, should wrestle with that doubt, saying the Lord's Prayer; and that she should be thus asking help for those who are dwelling in palaces, who scarcely dream of want, yet in their own way are in peril as great as hers; for the student, who in his chamber is haunted with questions which would seem to her monstrous and incredible, but which to him are agonizing; for the divine in his terrible assaults from cowardice, despondency, vanity, from the sense of his own heartlessness, from the shame of past neglect, from the appalling discovery of evils in himself which he has denounced in others, from vulgar outward temptations into which he had proudly fancied that he could not fall, from dark suggestions, recurring often, that words have no realities corresponding to them. . . . Of all this the sufferer knows nothing, yet for these she prays. . . . For one and all she cries, 'Lead us not into temptation!' Their temptations and hers, different in form, are alike in substance. They, like her, are tempted to doubt that God is, and that He is the Author of good and not of evil; and that He is mightier than the evil; and that He can and will overthrow it, and deliver the universe out of it. This is the real temptation; there is no other. . . . No man is out of the reach of it who is in God's world; no man is intended to be out of the reach of it who is God's child. He Himself has led us into this wilderness to be tempted of the devil; we cannot fly from it; . . . we cannot choose that we shall not have those temptations which are specially fitted to reach our own feelings, tempers, infirmities. . . . But we may cry, 'Lead us not into temptation;' and praying so, we pray against ourselves. . . . Praying so, that which seemed to be poison becomes medicine; . . . death itself is made the minister of life."

The sum of the whole doctrine of temptation is in this, — that it is the needful discipline of the immortal souL "Temptations," says a Roman Catholic writer, "are the raw material of glory." And every step of the long struggle, in which the higher gains the mastery over the lower, the spirit over the flesh, is a step onward and upward, at which we may well believe that the very angels of God raise songs of triumph.

I know, indeed, — ah! who does not? — by what slow degrees and toilsome and difficult ascent we struggle upward. I know the infinite evil if we fail. But shall we not still rejoice to be called to the solemn privilege which belongs to the children of God? Shall we go complaining all our days of the hardships which prove to us the *worth* of the soul educated at such a cost? No! if temptations are your lot in life — the school of trial which is the school of faith — you will go on resolved the more to wrestle with them till they disclose their heart of meaning, remembering that the Captain of our salvation was tried in the same furnace, was "made perfect through sufferings," was tempted and overcame.

True, it will be with "stumbling on the dark mountains," with outward fighting and inward fears, scarred and worn with the conflict, not unmarred by regrets and failures, and only by the grace of God at last, that we can gain "the prize of the high calling in Christ Jesus." But no dearer welcome is given to any who enter the kingdom of God, than that which awaits the faithful soul after such a struggle; and in the light of heaven the harsh experience of the past will be transfigured, — nay, rather, we shall see it as it really is.

"To him that overcometh," is the word of Christ, "will I grant to sit with me in my throne, even as I also overcame and am set down with my Father in His throne."

BUT DELIVER US FROM EVIL.

X.

BUT DELIVER US FROM EVIL.

But deliver us from evil. — MATT. vi. 13.

THIS is not merely a continuation of the prayer to be delivered from temptation. In that, as Mr. Maurice says, "a man prays against himself." But now he passes on to that which has been the instinctive cry of the human heart to whatever power it has worshipped, ever since men began to be, and felt the pressure and the agony of the countless ills of this troubled world. "For we know that the whole creation groaneth and travaileth in pain together until now. And not only they, but ourselves also, which have the first fruits of the Spirit, even we ourselves groan within ourselves."

We do not need to linger on any statement of what those ills are; we all know them. No cheerful optimism can banish them out of this world, or make them imaginary.

So then we can see how our Lord's Prayer should culminate in this final petition, "Deliver us from the evil that is so real." How can we be delivered? Only by laying hold on and being upheld by Him who is more real.

Men were tempted enough to let the evils shut out everything else from their sight. Therefore it is that our prayer began at the true beginning with the great thought of God, "Our Father," and it passed on to make His Name, His kingdom, His will supremely present to us before it trusted us to speak of our own needs at all. So now at last it brings us face to face with the problem of evil, with our minds full of the thought of God.

And when our minds are illuminated by that thought I think we all feel that every other evil seems small to us except that of sin and conscious wrong. It is *that* from which in our deepest prayer we pray to be set free. "O wretched man that I am, who shall deliver me from the body of this death?"

Our prayer reads in the Greek, ἀπὸ τοῦ πονηροῦ. The Revised Version translates it "the evil one." It ought to be said, if any are troubled by this, that it is a matter of grave dispute if the revisers have not gone too far. *The* evil may mean simply, in the neuter, to emphasize the intensity of the evil which oppresses us.

Our Saviour always either uses the language of the time on this subject, to impress some moral or spiritual truth, or in such a manner, in parables or figurative sayings, that it is hard measure if we tie them down as literal assertions. When Jesus speaks of the Evil One snatching away good seed from men's hearts; when he tells the Jews that they are "of their father, the Devil;" when he calls Peter Satan; when he speaks of "the Prince of this world," his language is not crusted into dogma, it is all alive. When he speaks of Belial or Beelzebub, he is using the very expressions with which the method of thought of his contemporaries is saturated, to convert them from their method of thought. "If *I* cast out demons thus, how do your children cast them out?" Saint Paul says that he has delivered certain persons "unto Satan, that they may learn not to blaspheme." If this was a literal statement, would it not be the very way to *teach* them to blaspheme instead of curing them? Saint Peter speaks of the Devil as "going about like a roaring lion, seeking whom he may devour;" is it a literal description, or a vivid figure?

It is very significant that when our Saviour speaks of the *origin of evil*, he says that it is in men's own hearts. As Saint Paul says, "Sin . . . deceived me and slew me." Yet these are the very statements in which we should have expected a clear announcement of the connection of the Evil Spirit with sin, if that tremendous idea, as often taught in the Church, be true.

The fatal flaw in the old Church doctrine was, that it made the Devil and not ourselves responsible, brought him in between the soul and God, and impaired the sense of dependence on our Heavenly Father, and the true faith in the redemption which is by Jesus Christ. It made the soul which God pleads with by his Holy Spirit, the prey of the wiles of the Lost Spirit. It made Jesus Christ's work an afterpiece to the Fiend's work, salvation a device for deliverance from the Enemy without, instead of regeneration within by Christ's spiritual strength. It required *faith in the* Devil, that is, in just that which we *cannot put faith in.* We must believe, then, in the infinitely Bad, in order to be assured of the infinitely Good; must lean on a rotten staff to be upheld, and cross a rotten plank over the abyss, in order to enter the kingdom of Heaven.

But all the more because we see that such a belief as this is pernicious, we should beware lest we make light of the solemn doctrine alike of reason and of Scripture, which the mediæval creed only feebly represented. That truth is that evil is a real power in the world, and that the lifelong contest with it may well try us to the uttermost; may overthrow us, save for the mighty succor of our God. Our foes in the Christian warfare are not mere external enemies, nor fleshly ills like hunger and pain; not even sorrow, loss, and separation pierce to the heart of this intense strife. The Christian doctrine of evil makes it far more than a vague abstraction; it is all quick with wicked life, incarnate in every wrong thought and thing, standing over against God. There is no more dangerous heresy of our time, none which more cuts the sinews of the moral fibre, than the idea that evil is mere weakness or ignorance, and not a deadly power, more active than a poison in the blood, more spreading than a weed in the ground. "Whether it be an *It* or a *Him* against whom we fight the battle of the Spirit, is of no consequence to us, human or divine. That evil is personal, directly our wills yield to it we know, and that the only refuge from it, the Divine Power which can alone deliver us, is personal, we also know. But that evil is personal before we absorb it into our own wills, we do not know, though we know that we should bear ourselves towards it exactly as if it were."

We in this church may have gained an advantage in the simplicity of our faith, by the omission of certain phrases in our Liturgy.

But we lose more than we gain if we fail to remember that the real enemies indicated by the words "the world, the flesh, and the Devil" beset us every hour. Père Ravignan once re-marked of the devils of the nineteenth century; "Messieurs, leur chef d'œuvre, c'est de s'être fait nier par ce siècle."

The sense of imperfection is profoundly bound up with the central thought of religion. I do not mean to say that religion centres in the doctrine of Sin; far otherwise, although it is sometimes so believed. But where the consciousness of Divine things is devout and strong, where the conscience is quick and sensitive to the call of duty, where God is felt to be present, and loyalty to Him is a living power in the soul, — there will be found a sober conviction of the woful falling-short that is in us. Not merely that we do not *know* our duty perfectly; that would be only short-sightedness; we would not be condemned for not seeing far. The inevitable limitations of our nature would not involve any moral quality of penal defect. Ignorance would not be guilt, but innocence. So far as it was really unconscious of moral obligation, that obligation would for it not exist.

We are well aware, however, that we fail to follow the law when we perceive it. Our knowledge is in no wise the measure of our service of it. Then follows in all high and thoughtful natures the humbling consciousness of weakness and imperfection. The first conviction that we have transgressed arises when we know, deep down in our souls, that we might have obeyed and knew enough to obey and ought to have obeyed, and failed to obey. This conviction is called forth, indeed, wherever there is a keen sense of the moral law; for such a sense is the way in which religion takes hold of many a man. When we apprehend the moral law we see a little way into the Being of God.

And yet this conviction is roused in its full intensity only when we pass beyond this impersonal presentation of duty to our minds, and see *the Lawgiver* behind the law. When we think of GOD, of the Power that holds the universe from falling into nothing, of the Goodness which our highest thought of holiness only faintly shadows forth, of the Truth that is reflected in absolute law of duty, of the Fatherly Love revealed to us by Jesus Christ, of all this as *personal* and *vital* in Him, — how poor and thin seems our best attainment!

That great Light pouring down into the very hiding-places of our weakness discloses it to our own startled sight. It is always the light which reveals the shadow.

But does it follow from this that the shadows are *only shadows*, with no substance in them? There are those who will tell you so; that this stern sense of our defect in the presence of the great thoughts of religion is a morbid excess of feeling, and that its true cure is to be found, not in efforts after an impossible perfection, nor yet in the soul's desire for communion with God, but simply in trying to live a plain, honest, peaceable life, without spiritual flights. But the soul has a deeper and a truer voice than this. It tells us that though the light does indeed *reveal* the shadows, it does not *make* them.

This is done by the light and a solid body together. Wherever there is a shadow, there is a substantial reality behind it, cutting off a certain portion of space from the light which overflows all around it. Sin — am I told ? — is merely a negative state, merely the absence of goodness! Is it then a statement which exhausts the matter, to say that *night* is only the absence of daylight? It is *that;* but what makes the daylight absent? When the strong mystery of the darkness wraps us round with its awful silences, broken only by the voices that come we know not how or whence, and the world lies dim and changed about us, and other worlds start out into the deep vaults of the sky with their pale fires that kindle answering lights of memory and reflection in the world within us, then that which veils us from the cheerful sun is not merely the emptiness of night; it is this very earth on which we stand. It is the shadow of that tremendous substantial fact, which projects its mighty cone of blackness off into the infinite spaces; and we call it night, though all the time the sun is shining as brightly as ever at the centre of the solar system; but the earth has come between us and his light. The very brightness of the sun makes the shadow more dark; the light and the earth conspire together to that end. And so with this question of moral evil. Will you say that it is a mere shadow of the fancy, the work of a morbid spirit, just as any man can make it dark for himself by shutting his own eyes even on the brightest day? But no! A universal phenomenon can be explained only by a substantial fact behind it. We cannot rationally suppose that the generality of mankind, from the beginning of history, have been thus misled, and that the highest and purest souls have been most misled. The shadow of moral evil has been felt among all races of men, so far as the light of any religion has been theirs. What does it indicate, if not that *the earth* with its passions and its evils came between them and the light, to make darkness?

We smooth over life, sometimes, till we smooth away all its meaning. The fact remains, from generation to generation, that human nature has its mingled substance of good and evil, and that it casts its shadow, long and dark, before the light of God's righteous law. If we loose our hold for a moment on the word which is associated with the church and religion, the word *Sin*, and take the word which carries practical religion into daily life, the word *Right*, the whole subject is at once *depolarized* for us. Right = that which is straight. A right line is the shortest distance between two points; there may be a million crooked ones, there can be but one which is straight. A right word is the only way to tell what is true; there can be a million lies, there can be but one truth. A right act is the straight way to obey God; there may be a million crooked paths of conduct, there can be only one straightforward one. By that plain rule of right do those Commandments written on yonder wall appeal to us, not as the *arbitrary* edict of God, but as formulating eternal laws of His own Being and of our being, given on Sinai, on tables of stone, but given also on tables of the human heart.

The long ages of the past accumulated a store of evils into which the children of the present have entered. History opens to us a record on whose pages is the trail of blood and the savor of wrong. The greed of neighbor against neighbor, the lusts of cruelty and injustice and revenge that are written there, we are tempted, in some moods of mind, to acknowledge to be our birth-wrong, — a law laid upon us by our fore-elders; and so we would fain hold them responsible for our defects of will and duty, deeming that we are bound with the chains of our fathers' sins.

Then, too, here we are in this world, not alone, but participants, whether we will or no, in what the French phrase terms the "solidarity of mankind." It is not more certain that the markets of the civilized world sympathize with one another, than it is that the morals of the civilized world are closely intertwined. This is the great distinction between the modern world and all the preceding centuries. Then men could shut themselves away in their village or their cell; at any rate, nations were insulated from one another. But now the delicate currents of thought and sympathy pass beneath all sundering seas.

Who can shut out, for example, the influences of the literature of his time? Though it swarm like the plagues of Egypt with disorder and disease, though the French novel be a dram of intellectual drunkenness, though the brilliant essay be sown thick with disbeliefs of the true and beautiful and good, we read in the name, forsooth, of *culture;* or, if we read not, the journals distil the gist of all into polished phrase, and those who seek the reputation of a *bel esprit*, dip in it the arrows of their repartee, and barb their winged wit with its poison.

Who can shut out the influences of the general tone of feeling about him? If the times are over eager in the pursuit of wealth, over giddy in that of pleasure, if the anchor of common thought fails to find holding ground on the deep seas of speculation, and the ship drifts with the wind, are we not all passengers?

Thus we release ourselves from personal responsibility for those things which we share with those about us. But there is a test, and a simple one, for our responsibleness. How goes the matter in our *secret spirit?* Does that answer willingly to the outside influences, or does it struggle against them? The evil is ours only when we *accept* it; as long as we wage even what seems a losing battle, the enemy is not master of the field. It is the secret sin which belongs to us, hid in our own hearts, which He sets in the light of His countenance.

Besides, the personal responsibility which is ours comes to us in ways which we cannot escape. We, respectable persons, of moral lives and good habits, what have we to do with the evil of the wicked world? We may answer with the apostle, "Much every way." A sin is often only the exaggeration of a virtue. It is necessary that a man should eat to live, but if he lives to eat, he falls into the sin of gluttony. Money is the means of life, but if he make life the means to money, he falls into the sin of avarice. Dress is the mark of a civilized being, but if we make our civilization to consist in fine clothes, we fall into the sin of luxury. And, more, it is even possible for us to keep within the moderate limit in our own judgment, and yet to add by example to the weight of evil influence that presses on another soul.

Here is a man of highest character, one of the leaders of public opinion, foremost in every good and generous thing. He is proud, as he has a right to be, of his good name. But he may use that pride to repel and to abase, and so may teach younger men the overbearing lesson which apart from his generous heart will make them one day grind the faces of the poor.

Here is one noted for austere honor. But one day a young man who has been educated to revere him, hears him point his conversation by a story of double meaning, or sees him bate his business principles to secure a bargain; and henceforth to that youth austere honor is but an empty shell.

Here is a woman who loves her church and holy things; but the trials to temper, or temptations to evil speech, do not come at church; they wait for her at home, where those who copy her pattern in larger letters, children and servants, study and lay to heart the *application* of her Christianity.

The fashion of our time is to fancy that vice can be expelled from the community by legislative enactment. "Begin at the outside, where we can see something, and work from that inwardly." Now doubtless much can be done in this way, if the enactment really expresses the honest moral sense of the community. For then it ceases to be a mere external force; it works with the moral weight of a whole people behind it. But the essential thing which we ought never to lose sight of is that no change is of permanent worth which does not substitute a holier spirit in place of the evil which it expels. You can really deliver from the evil only by inspiring with good.

And this is where the Christian prayer finds its answer in the Christian method. This is what the Gospel of Christ claims to do, and does, by giving motives and inspirations all its own.

My friends, there is always danger, when we discuss the great questions of Christian theology, lest we forget that they are not only matters of speculative interest, but have to do most immediately and urgently with the soul's very life. The theological statement is simply the best statement which men can make of the working out of spiritual truths by the soul. Nowhere is it more profoundly true than when we are dealing with the problem of evil, that we are tempted, when we speculate about it, to lose sight of the fact that it is all the time the most tremendous reality of life or of death, in their most intense form, *spiritual* life or *spiritual* death to others all around us. I am not of those who think that wickedness goes only with poverty and shabby clothes. There is plenty of it, in some forms, in the best society. All the sins which spring from self-indulgence and hardness of heart and selfishness can make themselves as much at home there as anywhere else. You do not know much about yourself if you have not yet learned that you can be tempted, and that temptation is a tremendous power, capable of shaking the soul to its very centre. But there is much in our way of life to protect us from some forms of evil, and amid the temptations to other forms of it to hide us from ourselves. So that, I say again, the danger is that for the most part our lives, easy, sheltered, sunny, prosperous, with love all about us and only pleasant looks in friendly faces, will lead us to forget what a battle is being fought all the time by other souls. To them the problem of evil is not a speculation; it is the question whether they can keep honest, temperate, truthful, manly; whether after falling, they can win their way back with struggle to some place far off and faintly resembling that fair place of innocence where they once stood.

I want to say to you, with all the solemnity of truth, that there is not one of us who can put off our whole responsibility in regard to these other children of God. We wrap ourselves in our own mantle of respectability, and are like men who should keep themselves warm beside the cheerful fire in a secure fortress, while they hear the wild beasts outside in the darkness where the belated traveller wanders. We are more responsible than we know for the lions that roar outside and for the fate of him whom they rend asunder. It is not well for us if we leave him who is fighting against the devil of drink, of impurity, of weakness, without a helping hand in his struggle. I am not preaching the condoning of wrong unrepented of, but a very different thing,—that we need to be quicker than we are to do what is the very work of heaven. For we are told that "there is joy among the angels of God over one sinner that repenteth." There is no doubt that if those who are comparatively safe from these evils will do their part, for example, simply to create and brace a public opinion to enforce the laws against intemperance, multitudes would be saved who now go down to the pit.

It comes home in another way. Is there one of us, mature men and women, who does not know some one who is trying, it may be weakly and fitfully, with that sense of previous defeat which takes away courage and faith, but still *trying* to put his tempter under his feet? Can you do nothing by a kind word and the grasp of a helping hand to make him strong? It is better to *do it* than by and by to cry, "Would God that I had known my opportunity before it was too late"!

I tell you, too, that there are those on whom the world looks coldly, and by their own fault, too, who are so fighting the devils in their own hearts and lives that they may be much more worthy of the "Well done" hereafter than those who live in placid self-content, never shaken by a great temptation, complacent in their own hearts, looking down on those who if they have greatly sinned have greatly repented, and never knowing how the soul scarred with defeat and bruised by sin may yet conquer by the grace of God.

Thus we have faced the fact that the evils against which we should supremely pray are those of Moral Evil. Yet we will not make light of the other things which we long to escape from. Here also we find refuge in the one thought of our God.

Our religion teaches us that God is Love. Faith in His love implies trust in His loving-kindness. But what kind of faith is that which can trust no further than it can see? Life is hard, you say; it bears painfully upon you. Be thankful still, and all the more be thankful, that you know that behind its stern seeming is this blessed Reality, the one ultimate ground of Christian Faith, the Living God, our Father in Christ Jesus. If, indeed, we may know Him as the Father, we can flee *from* Him by fleeing *to* Him; the darkest affliction will drive us to the Heart of the Mystery, which is God; and we shall find that we can rest the weary heart there in communion with Himself. It will be as in that passage of the ancient Scripture, only in a far higher and holier sense,— as when old Isaac lay blind from age and bowed with infirmity on his bed of sickness, he knew in the son whom he felt ministering to him in his needs, that though "the hands were the hands of Esau, the voice was the voice of Jacob." So, only more deeply and with more sacred meaning, the soul can hear, even when the touch that deals with it seems rough and strange, a Father's voice speaking words of cheer and peace. Not for the happiness of earth as thy being's end and aim, wast thou created, O child of God, but for that deeper joy, whose fruits of righteousness are won not without toil and pain! "Trial, like frost and snow, *kindly to the root*, though hurtful to the flower."

All these things are in the world, we know that they will be, yet we pray against them, and we do well. For we should remember that "men have not been praying in vain against it for six thousand years, but rather have been stemming, overcoming it continually; each of their prayers if offered in ever so much dimness and confusion, opening a vision out of the darkness." So then we can pray it, remembering always that *God* is better and stronger.

"By desiring what is perfectly good," says a great writer of our own time, "we are a part of the Divine power against evil, widening the skirts of light, and making the struggle with darkness narrower."

And though to none of us can it perfectly come in this world, that day of deliverance for which we pray, we know that it shall come at last. We have moments of that heaven *here*, of rest and trust and peace; and beyond, we have the assurance: "I shall be satisfied when I awake with Thy likeness."

Messrs. Roberts Brothers' Publications.

WAYS OF THE SPIRIT,

AND OTHER ESSAYS.

BY

FREDERIC HENRY HEDGE, D.D., LL.D.

The Way of History; The Way of Religion; The Way of Historic Christianity; The Way of Historic Atonement; The Natural History of Theism; Critique of Proofs of the Being of God; On the Origin of Things; The God of Religion, or the Human God; Dualism and Optimism; Pantheism; The Two Religions; The Mythical Element in the New Testament; Incarnation and Transubstantiation; The Human Soul.

SQUARE 12MO. CLOTH. PRICE $2.00.

Sold by all booksellers. Mailed, postpaid, by the Publishers,

ROBERTS BROTHERS, BOSTON.

Messrs. Roberts Brothers' Publications.

POSITIVE RELIGION.
ESSAYS, FRAGMENTS, AND HINTS.

By JOSEPH HENRY ALLEN,

Author of "Christian History in its Three Great Periods,"
"Hebrew Men and Times," etc.

16MO, CLOTH. PRICE, $1.25.

Among the subjects treated may be noted the following, viz.: "How Religions Grow," "A Religion of Trust," "The World-Religions," "The Death of Jesus," "The Question of a Future Life," "The Bright Side," "Religion and Modern Life," etc.

The subjects are discussed, as one will indeed plainly see, by a learned Christian scholar, and from that height in life's experience which one reaches at three score and ten years. They treat of the growth of religion; of religion as an experience; of the terms "Agnostic" and "God"; of the mystery of pain, of immortality and kindred topics. The author is among the best known of the older Unitarians, and the breadth of his views, together with his modesty of statement and ripeness of judgment, give the book a charm not too common in religious works. The literary style is also pleasing. — *Advertiser.*

This little volume of 260 pages contains much that is fresh and interesting and some things which are true only from a Unitarian standpoint. It is always delightful to read an author who knows what he is writing about, and can present his thoughts in a clear and forcible manner. His intention is to exhibit religion not so much "as a thing of opinion, of emotion, or of ceremony, as an element in men's own experience, or a force, mighty and even passionate, in the world's affairs." Such an endeavor is highly laudable, and the work has been well done. — *Christian Mirror.*

A collection of a acute, reverent, and suggestive talks on some of the great themes of religion. Many Christians will dissent from his free handling of certain traditional views, dogmas of Christianity, but they will be at once with him in his love of goodness and truth, and in his contention that religion finds its complete fruition in the lives rather than the speculative opinions of men. — *N. Y. Tribune.*

Mr. Allen strikes straight out from the shoulder, with energy that shows his natural force not only unabated, but increased with added years. "At Sixty: A New Year Letter" is sweet and mellow with the sunshine of the years that bring the philosophic mind. But we are doing what we said that we must not, and must make an arbitrary end. Yet not without a word of admiration for the splendid force and beauty of many passages. These are the product of no artifice, but are uniformly an expression of that humanity which is the writer's constant end and inspiration. In proportion as this finds free and full expression, the style assumes a warmth and color that not only give an intellectual pleasure, but make the heart leap up with sympathetic courage and resolve. — *J. W. C.*

Sold everywhere.

ROBERTS BROTHERS, PUBLISHERS.

Messrs. Roberts Brothers' Publications.

DAILY STRENGTH FOR DAILY NEEDS.

SELECTED BY THE EDITOR OF "QUIET HOURS."

16mo. Cloth, Price $1.00; white cloth, gilt, $1.25.

"This little book is made up of selections from Scripture, and verses of poetry, and prose selections for each day of the year. We turn with confidence to any selections of this kind which Mrs. Tileston may make. In her 'Quiet Hours,' 'Sunshine for the Soul,' 'The Blessed Life,' and other works, she has brought together a large amount of rich devotional material in a poetic form. Her present book does not disappoint us. We hail with satisfaction every contribution to devotional literature which shall be acceptable to liberal Christians. This selection is made up from a wide range of authors, and there is an equally wide range of topics. It is an excellent book for private devotion or for use at the family altar." — *Christian Register.*

"It is made up of brief selections in prose and verse, with accompanying texts of Scripture, for every day in the year, arranged by the editor of 'Quiet Hours,' and for the purpose of 'bringing the reader to perform the duties and to bear the burdens of each day with cheerfulness and courage.' It is hardly necessary to say that the selection is admirably made, and that the names one finds scattered through the volume suggest the truest spiritual insight and aspiration. It is a book to have always on one's table, and to make one's daily companion." — *Christian Union.*

"They are the words of those wise and holy men, who, in all ages, have realized the full beauty of spiritual experience. They are words to comfort, to encourage, to strengthen, and to uplift into faith and aspiration. It is pleasant to think of the high and extended moral development that were possible, if such a book were generally the daily companion and counsellor of thinking men and women. Every day of the year has its appropriate text and appropriate thoughts, all helping towards the best life of the reader. Such a volume needs no appeal to gain attention to it." — *Sunday Globe, Boston.*

Sold by all booksellers. Mailed, post-paid, on receipt of price, by the Publishers,

ROBERTS BROTHERS, BOSTON.

MARY W. TILESTON'S SELECTIONS.

Daily Strength for Daily Needs. Selections for every day
  in the year. 16mo. Plain $1.00
THE SAME. White, gilt 1.25
  "   " Padded calf 3.50
  "   "   " mor. 3.00
Sunshine in the Soul. Poems of Encouragement and Cheer-
  fulness. 16mo. Plain 1.00
THE SAME. White, gilt 1.25
  "   " Padded calf 3.50
  "   "   " mor. 3.00
First and Second Series, separately 50
Quiet Hours. A Collection of Poems. Square 16mo. First
  and Second Series, each 1.00
THE SAME. Two volumes in one. 16mo 1.50
  "   " White gilt 1.75
  "   " Flexible mor. 3.50
Sursum Corda. Hymns of Comfort. 16mo 1.25
The Blessed Life. Favorite Hymns. Square 18mo 1.00
Classic Heroic Ballads. 16mo. 1.00

WISDOM SERIES.

Issued in handsome pocket volumes. 18mo. Flexible covers,
red edges.

Selections from the Apocrypha $0.50
The Wisdom of Jesus, the Son of Sirach; or, Ecclesias-
  ticus 50
Selections from the Thoughts of Marcus Aurelius
  Antoninus 50
THE SAME. Mor., $1.50; calf 2.50
Selections from the Imitation of Christ 50
Selections from Epictetus 50
THE SAME. Mor., $1.50; calf 2.50
Selections from the Life and Sermons of Tauler . . .50
Selections from Fénelon 50
THE SAME. Mor., $1.50; calf 2.50
Socrates. The Apology and Crito of Plato 50
Socrates. The Phædo of Plato 50

Sold by all booksellers. Mailed, postpaid, on receipt of price.

ROBERTS BROTHERS, BOSTON.

Messrs. Roberts Brothers' Publications.

SUNSHINE IN THE SOUL

POEMS SELECTED BY THE EDITOR OF "QUIET HOURS."

———◆———

'Another delicate little *morceau* of a book. Seemly in its outer garb, but incomparably more beautiful within. A cunningly selected group, by the hand of a skilful arranger of poems, from the choicest writers. An exquisite and precious little book, that will doubtless let God's sunshine into many a sad soul." — *Christian Intelligencer.*

"'Sunshine in the Soul' is a collection, in a bijou volume, of a number of the most beautiful, tender, uplifting, and satisfying verses of a religious character which exist in our language. There is abundance of help and comfort in this little volume, and many a heart will be made glad in its possession." — *Boston Traveller.*

" Designed, as its title indicates, to cheer and elevate, and to be a bright companion for the reader. It is pleasant to find such a book of religious verse, that has nothing austere or gloomy in its pages, nothing that seems to darken heaven to man." — *Portland Press.*

———◆———

First and Second Series, 18mo, cloth. Price, 50 cents each. Both
series in one volume, price 75 cents. Sold by all Booksellers.
Mailed, postpaid, by the Publishers,

ROBERTS BROTHERS,
Boston

Messrs. Roberts Brothers' Publications.

EVERY-DAY LIFE AND EVERY-DAY MORALS.

By GEORGE LEONARD CHANEY.

16mo. Cloth. Price, $1.00.

A series of Discourses on the relation of Art, Business, the Stage, the Press, and the Pulpit, to Morals, as exemplified in Every-Day Work and Recreations.

In this fresh and charming volume, one who is well known and beloved in the churches of Boston sends back to New England a welcome greeting from "The Church of Our Father" in Atlanta. It speaks with the same voice which made the pulpit of Hollis-Street Church a power for practical religion during Mr. Chaney's most valuable ministry in this city, — a ministry which has left permanent results in not a little of the best denominational and philanthropic work which is done here. . . . The reader opens a series of chapters which lead him on through studies which touch all the great influences of modern social life in America. Fearless, frank, keen in their criticism of foibles, shams, and shames, they are lighted up by gleams of humor, and glow with the iridescent beauty of poetical imagination, while full of wise thought and noble motive. — *Christian Register.*

There are here eight pulpit discourses or addresses on "Art and Morals," "Juvenile Literature and Juvenile Morals," "Literature and Morals," "Industry and Morals," "Business and Morals," "The Stage and Morals," "The Press and Morals," "The Pulpit and Morals." They are full of strong, manly sense, wise discrimination, and noble. invigorating moral tone, expressed in a vivid and vigorous style that holds the reader from beginning to end. If it be true that the pulpit fails to attract, the fault is certainly not with such preachers as Mr. Chaney; for these discourses have in them intellectual fibre, the healthiest moral pulse, and the ring of downright honesty of speech of man to man, put in attractive form. If it be true that the pulpit deals with abstractions, that charge cannot be laid against these utterances, for the subjects are all of immediate interest, and are treated in a living way. For ourselves we find in Mr. Chaney's judgments little to dissent from. His opinions seem to us to be thoroughly sound, and his pages are studded with excellent and wholesome criticism and advice. The two addresses on "Juvenile Literature and Juvenile Morals" and "Literature and Morals" are wise helps to the young and to teachers of the young in the selection of their reading. The two lectures on the Stage and on the Press in their moral aspects are marked by balance and discrimination. The whole book is thoroughly breezy and bracing, and contains counsel of a noble, right-minded kind. — *The Unitarian Herald.*

Sold by all booksellers. Mailed, post-paid, on receipt of price, by the publishers,

ROBERTS BROTHERS, BOSTON.

Roberts Brothers' Publications.

ETHICAL RELIGION.

By WILLIAM MACKINTIRE SALTER.

12mo. Cloth. Price, $1.50.

A FEW CRITICAL OPINIONS.

One of the best and most useful books lately given to the public is "Ethical Religion," by WILLIAM MACKINTIRE SALTER, well known to all the leading thinkers in this country. The book, as stated in the preface, is made up of lectures given, for the most part, before the Society for Ethical Culture, of Chicago, and nowise claims to represent the movement, but simply reflects the author's own attitude of mind upon the various topics treated, namely: Ethical Religion, The Ideal Element in Morality, What is a Moral Action? Is there a higher Law? Is there anything Absolute about Morality? Darwinism in Ethics, The Social Ideal, The Rights of Labor, Personal Morality, On Some Features of the Ethics of Jesus, Do the Ethics of Jesus satisfy the Needs of our Time? Good Friday from a Modern Standpoint, The Success and the Failure of Protestantism, Why Unitarianism fails to satisfy, The Basis of the Ethical Movement, The Supremacy of Ethics, The True Basis of Religious Union. The author's style of writing is very charming, and what he says upon the various topics is said in a thoughtful and earnest way. It contains three hundred and thirty-two pages, printed on fine paper, and beautifully bound in cloth. The book deserves, and no doubt will have, a large sale. — *Truth.*

Here is the *soul* of religion. Here is the *living* worship. There are no husks here, true; but there are buds and blossoms in abundance and fragrance. There is here no "washing of cups and platters," granted; but there are here "the weightier matters of the law," — the eternal law of right. In a word, there is here, in glowing, suggestive epitome, the essence of true human being and doing. The world will not soon accept it all, especially as religion. It is not the sensuous, luxurious thing, the meretriciously upholstered and gaudily elaborate thing, the obstreperous, shouting, sense-satisfying thing that most people know as religion. But it is the religion of the heights and depths and innermost recesses; and if we read it well, we rise from it to stand erect and free as never before, — unless, indeed, we rise from it to fall upon our faces to hide ourselves from ourselves. — *The New Ideal.*

I especially thank you for Salter's book. I have read it with great profit, both as a philosopher and a man. Say to the author, if you think it will interest him, that I feel theoretically, as well as practically, benefited by his book. He lays down with great clearness, as well as exactness, the leading principles of philosophic ethics to his hearers and readers, and illustrates them by excellent and fitting examples from life, — the little every-day life, as well as the great historical life. And then the noble and pure spirit that pervades the entire book! It is in the true sense a book of edification. — *Letter from Prof. Harold Hoffding, of Copenhagen.*

And the foundation of the new religion? Morality! — of course, not that old morality which the Christian churches teach, but the real morality which, as Salter describes it, is something infinitely higher, is an independent idea, an independent law of the human spirit, is older than all convention and tradition and books and persons, and therefore able to overset and supplant them all. — *Evangelical Church Advertiser, Berlin.*

Sold by all booksellers.

ROBERTS BROTHERS, PUBLISHERS,

BOSTON, MASS.

Messrs. Roberts Brothers' Publications.

THE BLESSED LIFE.

Favorite Hymns selected by the Editor of " Quiet Hours," " Sursum Corda," " The Wisdom Series." 18mo, cloth, red edges. Price $1.00.

From the *Church Union.*

"This is a collection of more than two hundred hymns, all devotional, most of them familiar, being taken from current hymn-books of various religious orders, and wisely discriminated. Watts, Wesley, Doddridge, Baxter, and Cowper will live while the English tongue is spoken; and when that has perished, perchance the spirit which animated these beautiful hymns will survive, ever increasing in delightful harmony through endless ages."

From the *Inter-Ocean.*

" The author selects in this little volume some of the favorite hymns such as our mothers and grandmothers have loved and sung, as well as some of the more modern favorites, the object being to gather these old favorites into one small volume, suitable for the sick room or the quiet hours of rest. Many of them are grand and beautiful, and the world will be many hundred years older before the lips of men will sing any songs breathing more fervent devotion, or express in sweeter notes the worship of the soul. The author arranges them under the heads : ' Morning and Evening ; ' ' The Glory of the Lord ; ' ' Fervent in Spirit ; ' ' Serving the Lord ; ' ' Rejoicing in Hope ; ' ' Patient in Tribulation ; ' ' Trust in the Lord ; ' ' The Good Shepherd ; ' ' Within the Veil,' &c.

From *The Churchman.*

" ' The Blessed Life ' is a volume of favorite hymns, selected by the editor of ' Quiet Hours ' and ' Sursum Corda.' With a single exception, namely, Whittier's poem of ' The Eternal Goodness,' it is made up of selections from hymn-books prepared for worship, and contains, therefore, only such hymns as have been pronounced good by others besides the editor. It represents the best of those which have been judged better than ordinary."

Sold by all Booksellers. Mailed, post-paid, by the Publishers,

ROBERTS BROTHERS, BOSTON.

www.ingramcontent.com/pod-product-compliance
Lightning Source LLC
Chambersburg PA
CBHW031748230426
43669CB00007B/531